JUMBLE® GOLD

Strike It Rich with These Puzzles!

Henri Arnold,
Bob Lee,
Mike Argirion,
Jeff Knurek, &
David L. Hoyt

TRIUMPH
BOOKS

This book is available in quantity at special discounts
for your group or organization.

For further information, contact:

Triumph Books LLC
814 North Franklin Street
Chicago, Illinois 60610
Phone: (312) 337-0747
www.triumphbooks.com

Printed in U.S.A.

ISBN: 978-1-62937-354-6

Design by Sue Knopf

Contents

Classic Puzzles

1–25...Page 1

Daily Puzzles

26–160...Page 27

Challenger Puzzles

161–180...Page 163

Answers

Page 184

JUMBLE®

Gold

Classic Puzzles

JUMBLE®

Unscramble these four Jumbles, one letter to each square, to form four ordinary words.

ATAEB

CUPHO

SERYDS

BINGOX

Whoa! How can you be me? How did you get here?

I give up surgery and become a time traveler.

WHEN THE SURGEON MET HIMSELF IN A PARALLEL UNIVERSE, IT WAS A ----

Now arrange the circled letters to form the surprise answer, as suggested by the above cartoon.

Print answer here " ◯◯◯◯ - ◯ - ◯◯◯◯ "

2

JUMBLE®

Unscramble these four Jumbles, one letter to each square, to form four ordinary words.

NYORI

SYMUH

ROPSNE

COSETK

This is supposed to be done this week!

Cousin Eddie ordered the wrong wood and nails. When his truck gets fixed, we'll get it done.

THE STAIRCASE WASN'T GOING TO BE FINISHED ON SCHEDULE BECAUSE OF ALL THE ---

Now arrange the circled letters to form the surprise answer, as suggested by the above cartoon.

Print answer here

JUMBLE®

Unscramble these four Jumbles, one letter to each square, to form four ordinary words.

CLOFA

CIRLE

MURSEE

MIRPTE

The electric company is picking up logs today.

Great!

THEY RAISED CHICKENS AND GREW PINES ON THEIR ----

Now arrange the circled letters to form the surprise answer, as suggested by the above cartoon.

Print answer here "☐☐☐☐-☐☐☐☐" ☐☐☐☐

JUMBLE.

Unscramble these four Jumbles, one letter
to each square, to form four ordinary words.

HEWLE

KREYP

THOOSE

TAANSO

Happy 16th Birthday
Sydney!

Let's hold off
until the
other girls
get here.

May I open
my gifts
now?

THEY WOULD LET HER
OPEN HER BIRTHDAY GIFTS
AFTER EVERYONE ---

Now arrange the circled letters to form
the surprise answer, as suggested by the
above cartoon.

*Print
answer
here*

JUMBLE®

Unscramble these four Jumbles, one letter
to each square, to form four ordinary words.

GOSYG

PLIME

TOLUTE

AZEALB

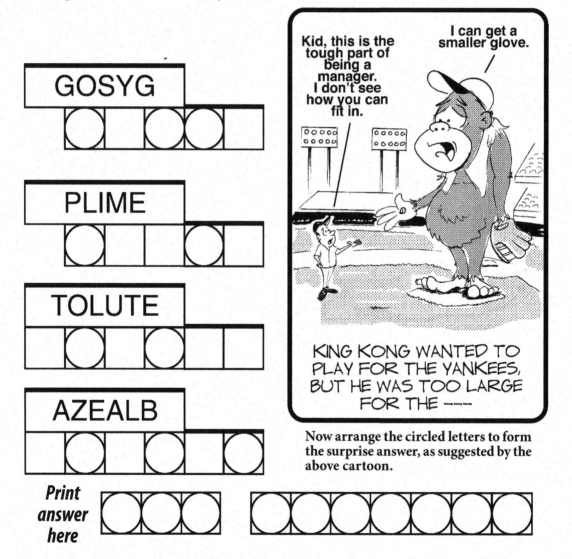

Kid, this is the
tough part of
being a
manager.
I don't see
how you can
fit in.

I can get a
smaller glove.

KING KONG WANTED TO
PLAY FOR THE YANKEES,
BUT HE WAS TOO LARGE
FOR THE ---

Now arrange the circled letters to form
the surprise answer, as suggested by the
above cartoon.

*Print
answer
here*

JUMBLE®

Unscramble these four Jumbles, one letter
to each square, to form four ordinary words.

LOVEW

MUDIH

SARYTA

BURCEH

We've never sold so
many so fast before.

THEY WERE SELLING
OUT OF BEATLES
ALBUMS IN ----

Now arrange the circled letters to form
the surprise answer, as suggested by the
above cartoon.

*Print
answer
here*

JUMBLE®

Unscramble these four Jumbles, one letter to each square, to form four ordinary words.

NYARI

KUSYH

MITURA

BLUMEH

I told you we have to pick paint colors today.

But...

HE TOLD HIS WIFE HE WAS GOING JOGGING, BUT HE SHOULD HAVE DONE THIS FIRST.

Now arrange the circled letters to form the surprise answer, as suggested by the above cartoon.

Print answer here

JUMBLE®

Unscramble these four Jumbles, one letter to each square, to form four ordinary words.

VEOBA

LEUFT

MICENO

GIDONI

How about we put the cartoon upside down?

Of course, you can't prank players.

JUMBLE

Players might flip out.

WHEN THEY DECIDED NOT TO PULL AN APRIL1 PRANK ON READERS, THEIR EDITOR SAID ---

Now arrange the circled letters to form the surprise answer, as suggested by the above cartoon.

Print answer here

PUZZLE
9

JUMBLE®

Unscramble these four Jumbles, one letter to each square, to form four ordinary words.

PEORA

UCETA

FRADYT

ASOSEN

That will be $4.00 each.

Are you crazy!? We're not paying to play at our park.

Mommy, I want to play!

PARK ADMISSION $4.00

PARKS & REC.

WHEN THE TOWN STARTED CHARGING TO USE THE PARK, IT WAS A ----

Now arrange the circled letters to form the surprise answer, as suggested by the above cartoon.

Print answer here " ◯◯◯ - ◯◯◯◯ "

10

JUMBLE®

Unscramble these four Jumbles, one letter
to each square, to form four ordinary words.

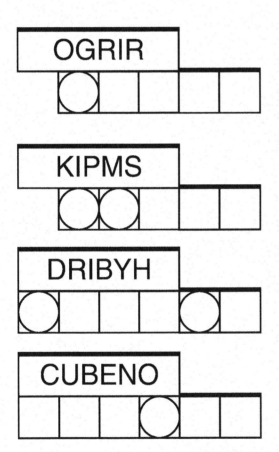

OGRIR

KIPMS

DRIBYH

CUBENO

People have been
listening to your
advice on the radio
and have stopped
coming to see me.

Go on.
I'm listening.

THE PSYCHIATRIST BEGAN
TO WORRY ABOUT HIS
BUSINESS AFTER IT
STARTED TO ---

Now arrange the circled letters to form
the surprise answer, as suggested by the
above cartoon.

Print answer here

JUMBLE®

Unscramble these four Jumbles, one letter
to each square, to form four ordinary words.

IGAME

LERDE

CIDPET

SNISIT

WHEN SHE BROWSED
THE INTERNET,
SHE WAS ----

Now arrange the circled letters to form
the surprise answer, as suggested by the
above cartoon.

*Print
answer
here* " ◯◯◯◯ " - ◯◯◯◯◯◯

JUMBLE®

Unscramble these four Jumbles, one letter
to each square, to form four ordinary words.

NALUN

BYRED

DUGLES

CIPTAM

How did you get here?

Now, what was I supposed to be scaring? What did you say?

THE SCARECROW DIDN'T HAVE A BRAIN, AND AS A RESULT WAS ---

Now arrange the circled letters to form
the surprise answer, as suggested by the
above cartoon.

*Print
answer
here*

⬡⬡⬡⬡⬡⬡ - ⬡⬡⬡⬡⬡⬡

JUMBLE®

Unscramble these four Jumbles, one letter
to each square, to form four ordinary words.

NODHU

RIEWP

GUDTER

ABEAMO

THE ARCHER WHO
THOUGHT HE WAS
THE BEST IN THE
WORLD WAS ----

Now arrange the circled letters to form
the surprise answer, as suggested by the
above cartoon.

Print answer
here   " ◯◯◯◯◯ - ◯◯◯◯ "

JUMBLE®

Unscramble these four Jumbles, one letter
to each square, to form four ordinary words.

ZAOKO

TUCHH

NORTGS

CREPOP

As you can see,
sales are really
starting to take off.

Sounds
great.

Looks
great.

TO PROJECT SALES OF
RECORD PLAYERS, THEY
USED ---

Now arrange the circled letters to form
the surprise answer, as suggested by the
above cartoon.

*Print
answer
here*

◯◯◯◯◯ - ◯◯◯◯◯◯

JUMBLE.

Unscramble these four Jumbles, one letter
to each square, to form four ordinary words.

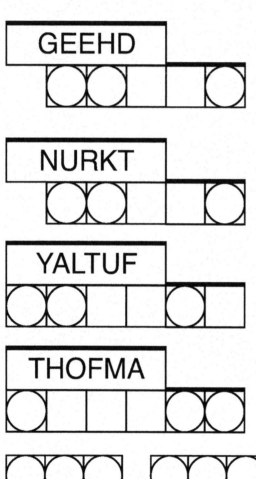

GEEHD

NURKT

YALTUF

THOFMA

I can't believe he got married.

His loss.

So, no more dating for you.

I'm fully invested in my marriage now.

AFTER THE STOCKBROKER
GOT MARRIED, HE WAS ----

Now arrange the circled letters to form
the surprise answer, as suggested by the
above cartoon.

Print answer here

JUMBLE®

Unscramble these four Jumbles, one letter
to each square, to form four ordinary words.

HYDAN

SLOFS

KRENBO

CARREH

You look so cute! I have to post this.

Gentlemen used to wear these all the time when I was young.

WHEN HE PUT ON HIS
GRANDFATHER'S HAT,
HE WAS ----

Now arrange the circled letters to form
the surprise answer, as suggested by the
above cartoon.

*Print answer
here* " "

JUMBLE®

Unscramble these four Jumbles, one letter to each square, to form four ordinary words.

PURET

OTABU

MURMYC

HNUYCK

Is she even going to talk to you?

First, I'll send her roses. Then, pick her up by limo. Then, we'll go out for dinner.

THE QB'S GIRLFRIEND BROKE UP WITH HIM, BUT HE WAS GOING TO TRY TO ---

Now arrange the circled letters to form the surprise answer, as suggested by the above cartoon.

Print answer here

JUMBLE®

Unscramble these four Jumbles, one letter to each square, to form four ordinary words.

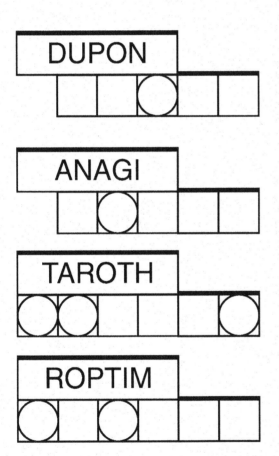

DUPON

ANAGI

TAROTH

ROPTIM

When was the last time you wore this?

Oh, no! I can't even move in this.

AFTER SEEING HOW SNUG HER DRESS HAD BECOME, SHE WAS ---

Now arrange the circled letters to form the surprise answer, as suggested by the above cartoon.

Print answer here

JUMBLE

Unscramble these four Jumbles, one letter
to each square, to form four ordinary words.

PUNTI

GEWIH

RAPURO

TENNIY

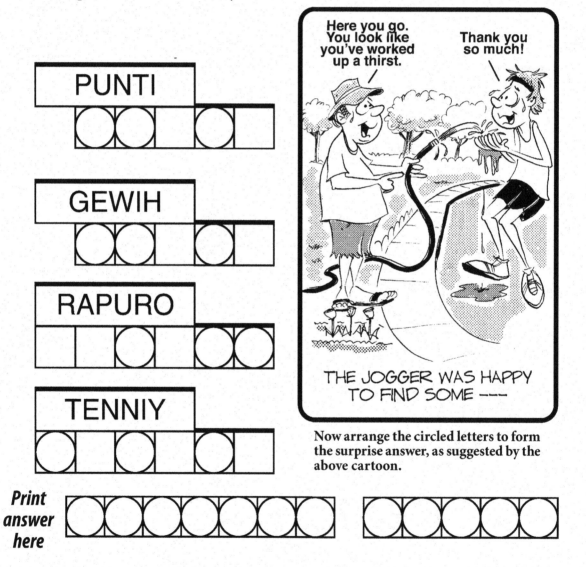

Here you go.
You look like
you've worked
up a thirst.

Thank you
so much!

THE JOGGER WAS HAPPY
TO FIND SOME ---

Now arrange the circled letters to form
the surprise answer, as suggested by the
above cartoon.

*Print
answer
here*

JUMBLE®

Unscramble these four Jumbles, one letter to each square, to form four ordinary words.

BURGY

NUGTS

HURNCC

CADIVE

WELCOME TO JELLYSTONE!

Yogi! Come here! You've gotten so big. What have you been eating?

Yikes! Hi, Auntie. Boy, you're strong.

YOGI'S FAMILY REUNION FEATURED ---

Now arrange the circled letters to form the surprise answer, as suggested by the above cartoon.

Print answer here

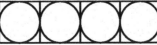 

21

JUMBLE®

Unscramble these four Jumbles, one letter to each square, to form four ordinary words.

WORNC

ENHOY

NELLOY

TIKENT

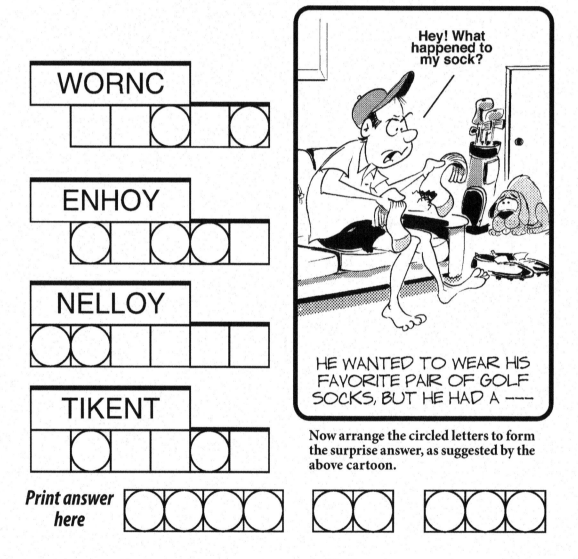

Hey! What happened to my sock?

HE WANTED TO WEAR HIS FAVORITE PAIR OF GOLF SOCKS, BUT HE HAD A ----

Now arrange the circled letters to form the surprise answer, as suggested by the above cartoon.

Print answer here

JUMBLE®

Unscramble these four Jumbles, one letter
to each square, to form four ordinary words.

CIEEN

ATEBA

DONEET

KERBOR

That's it! You're out of here! And never come back!

AFTER THE ROCK GROUP TRASHED THEIR HOTEL SUITE, THEY WERE ----

Now arrange the circled letters to form the surprise answer, as suggested by the above cartoon.

Print answer here

23

JUMBLE®

Unscramble these four Jumbles, one letter
to each square, to form four ordinary words.

SPATN

TVOID

GARFOE

SUMEIS

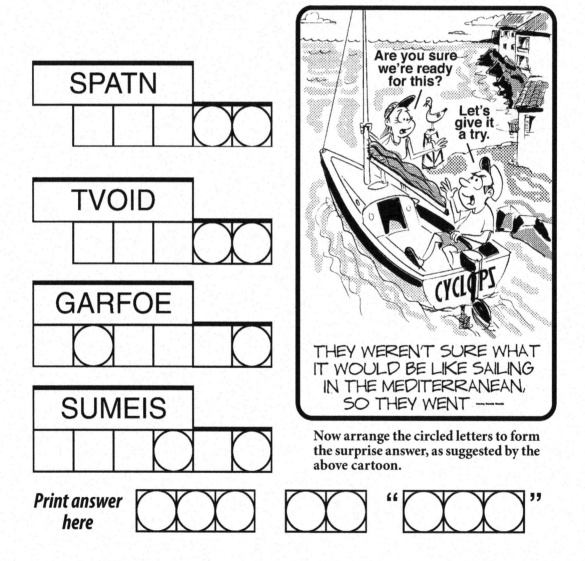

Are you sure
we're ready
for this?

Let's
give it
a try.

CYCLOPS

THEY WEREN'T SURE WHAT
IT WOULD BE LIKE SAILING
IN THE MEDITERRANEAN,
SO THEY WENT ———

Now arrange the circled letters to form
the surprise answer, as suggested by the
above cartoon.

**Print answer
here** ⬜⬜⬜ ⬜⬜ " ⬜⬜⬜ "

JUMBLE ®

Unscramble these four Jumbles, one letter
to each square, to form four ordinary words.

SPERS

SOPIE

OXTERV

BENKOR

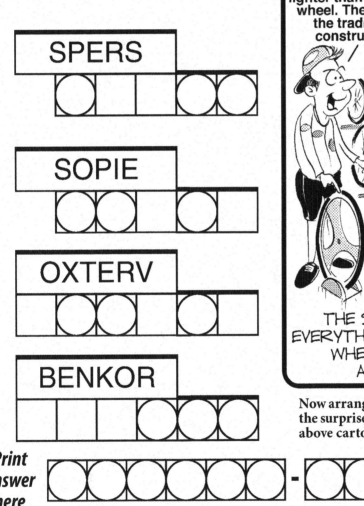

Now, this one is lighter than any other wheel. The other is the traditional construction.

Wow! You know your wheels.

THE SALESMAN KNEW
EVERYTHING ABOUT BICYCLE
WHEELS AND MADE
A GREAT ---

Now arrange the circled letters to form
the surprise answer, as suggested by the
above cartoon.

Print answer here

JUMBLE®

Unscramble these four Jumbles, one letter
to each square, to form four ordinary words.

SIDYA

RASHH

DEPIME

KHNIRS

Here you go.
I'll take the
convertible home.

Why do I
always
have to
drive the
work car?

THE HUSBAND AND WIFE
WHO OWNED THE FUNERAL
HOME HAD TWO CARS, ----

Now arrange the circled letters to form
the surprise answer, as suggested by the
above cartoon.

*Print
answer
here*

JUMBLE® Gold

Daily Puzzles

JUMBLE®

Unscramble these four Jumbles, one letter to each square, to form four ordinary words.

TOIDI

HOSEV

MERITH

DECAFA

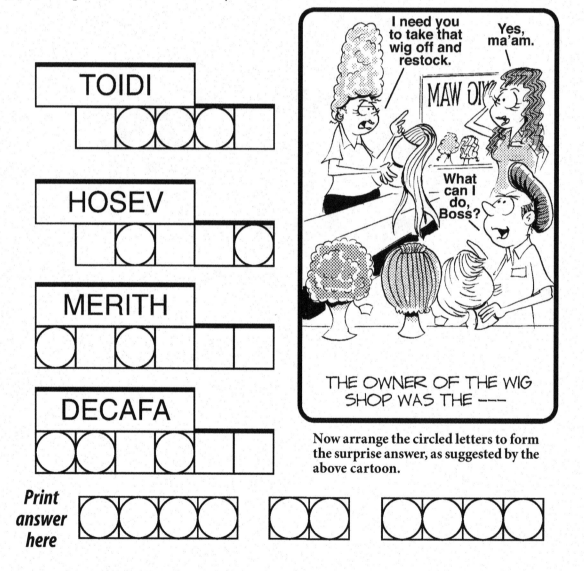

THE OWNER OF THE WIG SHOP WAS THE ---

Now arrange the circled letters to form the surprise answer, as suggested by the above cartoon.

Print answer here

JUMBLE®

Unscramble these four Jumbles, one letter
to each square, to form four ordinary words.

ULFID

FRAWE

THINCS

GAVEYO

He always
wins this
event.

He's
just a
natural.

A POPULAR EVENT AT THE
WATERFOWL OLYMPICS
WAS THE ---

Now arrange the circled letters to form
the surprise answer, as suggested by the
above cartoon.

Print answer here

29

JUMBLE®

Unscramble these four Jumbles, one letter
to each square, to form four ordinary words.

SADIY

SAAIL

LUTOND

FROFET

I'm stumped. Did you finish the Jumble already?

Christie, I'll give you a clue to help you get the answer.

WHEN SHE HAD TROUBLE
SOLVING THE JUMBLE,
ASKING HER FATHER FOR
HELP WAS THE ---

Now arrange the circled letters to form
the surprise answer, as suggested by the
above cartoon.

Print answer here

JUMBLE®

Unscramble these four Jumbles, one letter to each square, to form four ordinary words.

PODTA

SALCH

BUDEOL

HYLTIF

Now, you're the princess and you're a frog. Here are your lines...

I'm not kissing him.

Should I jump around?

WHEN SHAKESPEARE WAS A KID, PUTTING ON A PERFORMANCE WAS ---

Now arrange the circled letters to form the surprise answer, as suggested by the above cartoon.

Print answer here

JUMBLE.

Unscramble these four Jumbles, one letter
to each square, to form four ordinary words.

IMTIL

NOGIG

SENUUR

LOFRAM

When it's my turn, I'm going to sing, "Don't Stop Believing."

'Cause if you liked it, then you should have put a ring on it

Ladies Night Karaoke

'Cause if you liked it, then you should have put a ring on it

THE LADIES LINED UP TO
SING KARAOKE ----

Now arrange the circled letters to form
the surprise answer, as suggested by the
above cartoon.

*Print
answer
here* "⬡⬡⬡⬡⬡ - ⬡⬡⬡" ⬡⬡⬡⬡

JUMBLE®

Unscramble these four Jumbles, one letter
to each square, to form four ordinary words.

SSEEN

TRUBL

EUNNOR

WALLUF

Whoa! Come back here.

Why won't he stay in the barn?

THE OUT-OF-CONTROL HORSE WAS ---

Now arrange the circled letters to form
the surprise answer, as suggested by the
above cartoon.

Print answer here ◯◯ - ◯◯◯◯◯◯◯

JUMBLE®

Unscramble these four Jumbles, one letter
to each square, to form four ordinary words.

PBMIL

TANGI

PRNUSG

DERCUE

I'd like to buy that building.
It has a great view of the city.

Will that
be cash?

AFTER HE WON THE
LOTTERY, KING KONG
BECAME A ----

Now arrange the circled letters to form
the surprise answer, as suggested by the
above cartoon.

*Print
answer
here*

JUMBLE®

Unscramble these four Jumbles, one letter
to each square, to form four ordinary words.

RUSTM

VECOT

AMSEES

KUREEB

I'm so sorry. I was trying to get away from the paparazzi.

OLLYWOOD

Brad Pitt! I...I...you... uh...

AFTER BUMPING INTO THE CELEBRITY ON THE STREET, SHE WAS ---

Now arrange the circled letters to form
the surprise answer, as suggested by the
above cartoon.

Print answer here ◯◯◯◯ - ◯◯◯◯◯◯

JUMBLE®

Unscramble these four Jumbles, one letter
to each square, to form four ordinary words.

KINTH

POTIV

ROPRAL

POXSEE

That was a nice
warm-up.

Wow! That
was fast.

THE MOUNTAIN CLIMBER
WHO REACHED THE PEAK
FIRST WAS IN ---

Now arrange the circled letters to form
the surprise answer, as suggested by the
above cartoon.

*Print
answer
here*

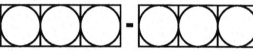

JUMBLE®

Unscramble these four Jumbles, one letter
to each square, to form four ordinary words.

FEHTT

NALTS

RAPYAL

DEMLID

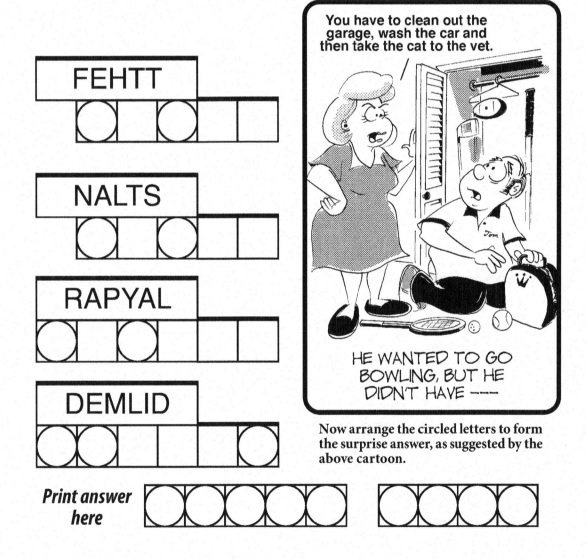

You have to clean out the
garage, wash the car and
then take the cat to the vet.

HE WANTED TO GO
BOWLING, BUT HE
DIDN'T HAVE ----

Now arrange the circled letters to form
the surprise answer, as suggested by the
above cartoon.

*Print answer
here*

PUZZLE
36

JUMBLE®

Unscramble these four Jumbles, one letter
to each square, to form four ordinary words.

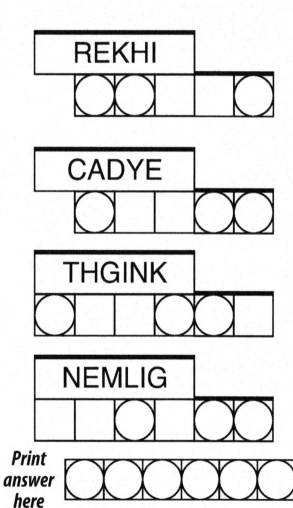

REKHI

CADYE

THGINK

NEMLIG

**Print
answer
here**

Nice match,
private.

Fort Hoyt Tennis Tourney

I see why you're
No. 1, general.

GEN. 6 6
2 2

THE ARMY GENERAL WHO
PLAYED IN THE TENNIS
TOURNAMENT WAS ----

Now arrange the circled letters to form
the surprise answer, as suggested by the
above cartoon.

38

JUMBLE®

Unscramble these four Jumbles, one letter
to each square, to form four ordinary words.

DUNOW

LONEV

MODDEO

SENNUK

Look at those idiots.

They don't get anywhere fast.

WHAT SNOBBY
BIRDS WITH BIG
EGOS DO.

Now arrange the circled letters to form
the surprise answer, as suggested by the
above cartoon.

Print answer here

39

JUMBLE®

Unscramble these four Jumbles, one letter to each square, to form four ordinary words.

NEESS

ADEGA

TREELT

CLEDOK

Coach, what were you thinking when you were down by 70 at the half?

WHEN IT CAME TIME TO EXPLAIN THE TEAM'S DEFEAT, THE COACH WAS THIS.

Now arrange the circled letters to form the surprise answer, as suggested by the above cartoon.

Print answer here

JUMBLE®

Unscramble these four Jumbles, one letter
to each square, to form four ordinary words.

SCAIB

AASIL

LUYGIT

RONUDA

I'm outta here.

DOUBLE JUMBLE   JUMBLE COLA

000000 20 0000 0013
0000000 020 000000 2

THE UMPIRE WAS GLAD
THE GAME WAS FINALLY
OVER BECAUSE HE WAS
READY TO ---

Now arrange the circled letters to form
the surprise answer, as suggested by the
above cartoon.

*Print
answer
here*

JUMBLE.

Unscramble these four Jumbles, one letter
to each square, to form four ordinary words.

VEGIN

ZOWOY

TEDYUP

LABTEL

Bring in the
UFO. Alien,
you're on.
Action!

THE MOVIE SET IN
DEATH VALLEY
HAD A ---

Now arrange the circled letters to form
the surprise answer, as suggested by the
above cartoon.

*Print answer
here*

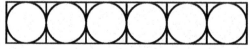

JUMBLE®

Unscramble these four Jumbles, one letter to each square, to form four ordinary words.

RANGL

GINIC

LAFTUR

NEETIC

I hope I get this right and get hired.

WHEN THE GUITARIST AUDITIONED FOR THE BAND, HE WAS ---

Now arrange the circled letters to form the surprise answer, as suggested by the above cartoon.

Print answer here " ⬡⬡⬡⬡⬡⬡⬡⬡ "

43

JUMBLE®

Unscramble these four Jumbles, one letter
to each square, to form four ordinary words.

POCAN

GLIYN

HOKOUN

NIRFIM

...and furthermore...

Time.

THIS COMES OUT
DURING A DEBATE.

Now arrange the circled letters to form
the surprise answer, as suggested by the
above cartoon.

Print
answer
here

JUMBLE®

Unscramble these four Jumbles, one letter
to each square, to form four ordinary words.

KAQUE

IGSEE

YULIBS

INNEAC

I raise.

WHAT THE POKER
PLAYER HAD WHEN THE
ROYALS JOINED
THE GAME.

Now arrange the circled letters to form
the surprise answer, as suggested by the
above cartoon.

**Print
answer
here**

AND

JUMBLE®

Unscramble these four Jumbles, one letter
to each square, to form four ordinary words.

WHYSO
◯◯◯☐

TELIE
☐◯☐◯

LADPIL
◯◯☐☐◯

LUSHIM
☐◯☐◯◯

Looks like a parking lot down there. Nothing's moving.

WHAT THE TRAFFIC
REPORTER SAID WHEN
THE POLICE CHASE
TIED UP THE ROADS.

Now arrange the circled letters to form
the surprise answer, as suggested by the
above cartoon.

**Print
answer
here**   " ◯◯ ' ◯ A ◯◯◯◯◯◯◯ "

JUMBLE®

Unscramble these four Jumbles, one letter
to each square, to form four ordinary words.

DICHE

TOUHY

CLARGI

YEMITS

Give the lady
your card

It looks good
on you

WHAT HE GOT WHEN
HIS WIFE BOUGHT
THE DESIGNER
DRESS.

Now arrange the circled letters to form
the surprise answer, as suggested by the
above cartoon.

**Print answer
here** ◯◯◯ " ◯◯◯◯◯◯ "

47

JUMBLE®

Unscramble these four Jumbles, one letter
to each square, to form four ordinary words.

OJYLL

PARVO

BYRBAC

FLUTIE

You would never
know he was once
down and out

THE VERY TOP
CAN BE ACHIEVED
FROM THIS.

Now arrange the circled letters to form
the surprise answer, as suggested by the
above cartoon.

Print answer here

JUMBLE®

Unscramble these four Jumbles, one letter
to each square, to form four ordinary words.

DEVEL

CHITK

EMBACE

YODMEB

This is the
last one

Another job
well done

WHAT THE IRON-
WORKERS DID WHEN
THEY BUILT THE
TOWER.

Now arrange the circled letters to form
the surprise answer, as suggested by the
above cartoon.

*Print
answer
here*   " "

49

JUMBLE®

Unscramble these four Jumbles, one letter to each square, to form four ordinary words.

LAFAT

IDDEA

PLAACA

REESOI

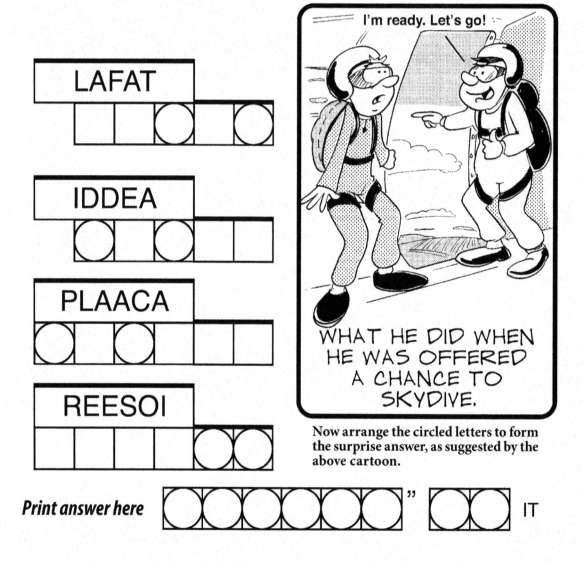

I'm ready. Let's go!

WHAT HE DID WHEN HE WAS OFFERED A CHANCE TO SKYDIVE.

Now arrange the circled letters to form the surprise answer, as suggested by the above cartoon.

Print answer here ⬡⬡⬡⬡⬡⬡ " ⬡⬡ IT

JUMBLE

Unscramble these four Jumbles, one letter to each square, to form four ordinary words.

SOBAS

KLANE

CUNBOE

GITSAM

Some days are better than others

THE HIGH ROLLER LEFT THE CASINO WITH A SMALL FORTUNE BECAUSE HE ---

Now arrange the circled letters to form the surprise answer, as suggested by the above cartoon.

Print answer here

[ ][ ][ ][ ] A [ ][ ][ ] [ ][ ][ ]

JUMBLE®

Unscramble these four Jumbles, one letter
to each square, to form four ordinary words.

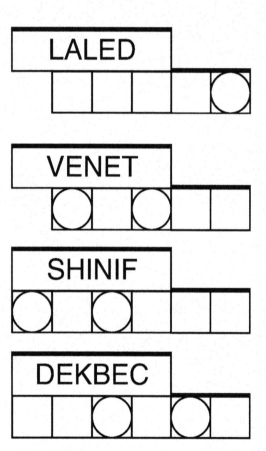

LALED

VENET

SHINIF

DEKBEC

We'll never break out of here

WHAT BARBED
WIRE IS USUALLY
USED FOR.

Now arrange the circled letters to form
the surprise answer, as suggested by the
above cartoon.

Print answer here

52

JUMBLE®

Unscramble these four Jumbles, one letter
to each square, to form four ordinary words.

NAHVE

LEGYE

NAHDEL

CLAMIE

This is
very heavy

WHAT THE
APPRENTICE DID FOR
THE CLOCKMAKER.

Now arrange the circled letters to form
the surprise answer, as suggested by the
above cartoon.

*Print
answer
here*

A " "

JUMBLE®

Unscramble these four Jumbles, one letter
to each square, to form four ordinary words.

THRIM

FOREY

RAYPNT

CHOROT

HIS READING OF
SONNETS ON THE
TRAIN WAS KNOWN
AS THIS.

Now arrange the circled letters to form
the surprise answer, as suggested by the
above cartoon.

Print answer here

IN

JUMBLE®

Unscramble these four Jumbles, one letter
to each square, to form four ordinary words.

MAGLE

GIERT

GANBIK

TAYRRM

How do you know
the right amount?

HOW HAND-ME-
DOWN RECIPES
ARE MEASURED.

Now arrange the circled letters to form
the surprise answer, as suggested by the
above cartoon.

*Print
answer
here* " ◯◯◯◯ " ◯◯ " ◯◯◯◯ "

JUMBLE®

Unscramble these four Jumbles, one letter to each square, to form four ordinary words.

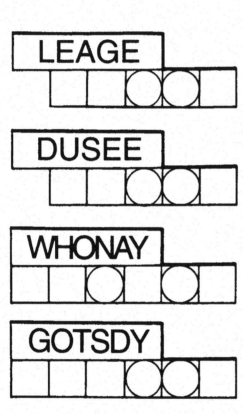

LEAGE

DUSEE

WHONAY

GOTSDY

Sit! Pay attention! Sit!

She certainly keeps trying

HOW SHE PURSUED HER PET'S OBEDIENCE TRAINING.

Now arrange the circled letters to form the surprise answer, as suggested by the above cartoon.

Print answer here

56

JUMBLE®

Unscramble these four Jumbles, one letter
to each square, to form four ordinary words.

ZUZYF

ROWEB

TONTUB

DACAFE

How dare you raise the rates!

WHAT SHE THOUGHT
OF THE AIRLINE'S
PRICE INCREASE.

Now arrange the circled letters to form
the surprise answer, as suggested by the
above cartoon.

Print answer here ⬡⬡ – ⬡⬡⬡⬡ !

57

JUMBLE®

Unscramble these four Jumbles, one letter to each square, to form four ordinary words.

COPAH

JEECT

HAVEEB

HIRTTY

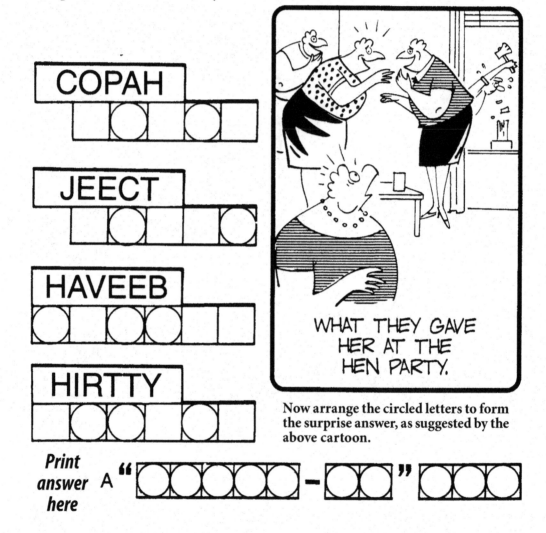

WHAT THEY GAVE
HER AT THE
HEN PARTY.

Now arrange the circled letters to form the surprise answer, as suggested by the above cartoon.

Print answer here

A " ☐☐☐☐☐ – ☐☐ " ☐☐☐

JUMBLE®

Unscramble these four Jumbles, one letter
to each square, to form four ordinary words.

HECEL

MUBIE

RAFTLE

FRUIPY

Someone stole
the herd!

They went
thataway!

ANOTHER NAME FOR
A CATTLE RUSTLER.

Now arrange the circled letters to form
the surprise answer, as suggested by the
above cartoon.

Print answer here A ☐☐☐☐☐ ☐☐☐☐☐☐

JUMBLE®

Unscramble these four Jumbles, one letter
to each square, to form four ordinary words.

YOHBB

YAGUD

TIFFUL

CLUNUR

HOW THE TILING
CHORE LEFT HIM.

Now arrange the circled letters to form
the surprise answer, as suggested by the
above cartoon.

Print answer here " ⬡⬡⬡⬡⬡ – ⬡⬡⬡ "

60

JUMBLE®

Unscramble these four Jumbles, one letter
to each square, to form four ordinary words.

HELEW

TARDF

RYCKIT

TYNTOK

WHAT THE HAMLET
CALLED THE NEW
ARRIVAL.

Now arrange the circled letters to form
the surprise answer, as suggested by the
above cartoon.

Print answer here   THE ⬡⬡⬡⬡ ⬡⬡⬡⬡⬡

JUMBLE®

Unscramble these four Jumbles, one letter
to each square, to form four ordinary words.

FYMIL

OSSUE

GAMENT

UPBRAL

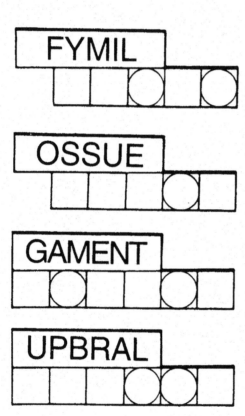

SHE WAS UNANIMOUSLY
CHOSEN QUEEN
BECAUSE THE JUDGES
GAVE HER THIS.

Now arrange the circled letters to form
the surprise answer, as suggested by the
above cartoon.

Print answer here

JUMBLE®

Unscramble these four Jumbles, one letter to each square, to form four ordinary words.

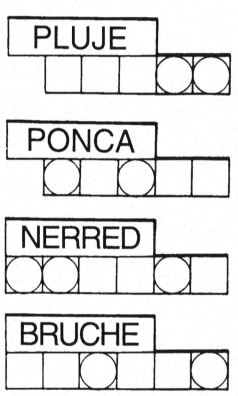

PLUJE

PONCA

NERRED

BRUCHE

I could crawl to work faster than this

WHAT THE COMMUTERS CALLED THE DAILY TRAFFIC JAM.

Now arrange the circled letters to form the surprise answer, as suggested by the above cartoon.

Print answer here

JUMBLE®

Unscramble these four Jumbles, one letter
to each square, to form four ordinary words.

SPAWM

GUBYL

MEEDER

JALOCE

We
lost
again

We'll
win the
next one

COA

IN DEFEAT, A BALL
GAME CAN TURN
INTO THIS.

Now arrange the circled letters to form
the surprise answer, as suggested by the
above cartoon.

Print answer here A ◯◯◯◯◯ ◯◯◯◯◯

JUMBLE ®

Unscramble these four Jumbles, one letter
to each square, to form four ordinary words.

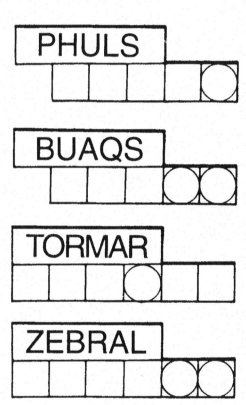

PHULS

BUAQS

TORMAR

ZEBRAL

Whew! I must have dropped
a few pounds

Are
you
OK?

WHAT THE
WINNING MARATHON
RUNNER LOST.

Now arrange the circled letters to form
the surprise answer, as suggested by the
above cartoon.

Print answer here   HER

JUMBLE®

Unscramble these four Jumbles, one letter to each square, to form four ordinary words.

MAFER

FETAC

FEENAD

GOFORT

Let's merge our personal portfolios

WHAT SHE CALLED THE STOCKBROKER'S PROPOSAL

Now arrange the circled letters to form the surprise answer, as suggested by the above cartoon.

Print answer here

A " ⬡⬡⬡⬡⬡⬡ " ⬡⬡⬡⬡⬡

PUZZLE
65

JUMBLE®

Unscramble these four Jumbles, one letter
to each square, to form four ordinary words.

NAWGO

LECEX

TRIAFY

HACCTY

Tsk! Tsk!

WHAT LATE SNACKS
GIVE A DIET.

Now arrange the circled letters to form
the surprise answer, as suggested by the
above cartoon.

Print answer here A ⬡⬡⬡ ⬡⬡⬡⬡⬡⬡

67

JUMBLE®

Unscramble these four Jumbles, one letter
to each square, to form four ordinary words.

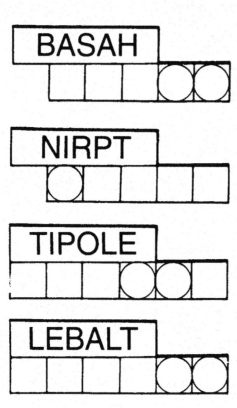

BASAH

NIRPT

TIPOLE

LEBALT

Whew! What
a relief!

WHAT THE MINERS
CONSIDERED THEIR
WORKPLACE.

Now arrange the circled letters to form
the surprise answer, as suggested by the
above cartoon.

Print answer here

JUMBLE®

Unscramble these four Jumbles, one letter
to each square, to form four ordinary words.

KWISH

PYTEM

CUTOCL

DULBOY

I tried to date her, but she
said she didn't like me

Me,
too

WHY THE
GUITARIST NEVER
GOT MARRIED.

Now arrange the circled letters to form
the surprise answer, as suggested by the
above cartoon.

Print answer here SHE
WAS ⬡⬡⬡ " ⬡⬡⬡⬡⬡ "

JUMBLE®

Unscramble these four Jumbles, one letter
to each square, to form four ordinary words.

LIVIG

SELLI

ALOONG

PENMAD

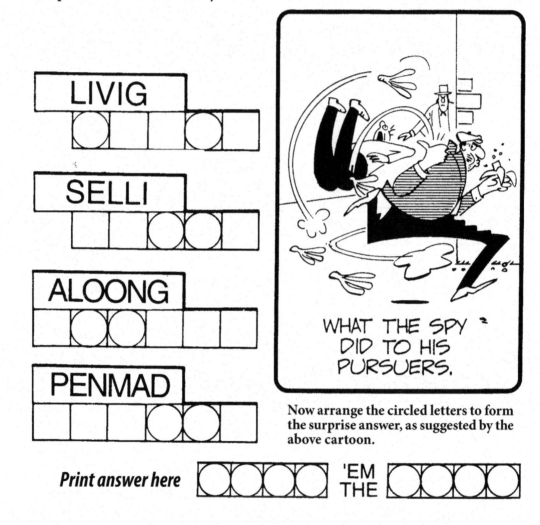

WHAT THE SPY
DID TO HIS
PURSUERS.

Now arrange the circled letters to form
the surprise answer, as suggested by the
above cartoon.

Print answer here ⬡⬡⬡⬡ 'EM THE ⬡⬡⬡⬡

JUMBLE®

Unscramble these four Jumbles, one letter to each square, to form four ordinary words.

GYKAW

CORUC

SATECK

BELBUB

I understand they don't make much

WHAT COWBOYS GET FOR RIDING BRONCOS.

Now arrange the circled letters to form the surprise answer, as suggested by the above cartoon.

Print answer here A ⬡⬡⬡⬡⬡ OR ⬡⬡⬡

JUMBLE®

Unscramble these four Jumbles, one letter
to each square, to form four ordinary words.

AGELL

WARLD

DREHSW

RESOOM

Step it up!

HOW THE DRESS-
MAKERS DESCRIBED
THEIR STERN BOSS.

Now arrange the circled letters to form
the surprise answer, as suggested by the
above cartoon.

Print answer here A ☐☐☐☐ AND ☐☐☐☐

JUMBLE®

Unscramble these four Jumbles, one letter
to each square, to form four ordinary words.

THACC

NEKIF

DIMPER

NAILET

What a
stupid move!

Look who's
talking

WHEN THE CHESS
GAME ENDED IN A
DRAW THEY WERE----

Now arrange the circled letters to form
the surprise answer, as suggested by the
above cartoon.

Print answer here ☐☐☐ TO ☐☐☐☐
BE

73

JUMBLE®

Unscramble these four Jumbles, one letter
to each square, to form four ordinary words.

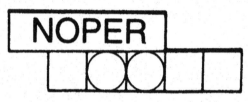

NOPER

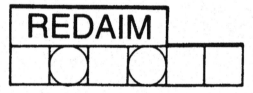

JONEY

REDAIM

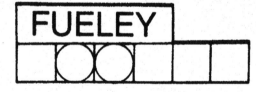

FUELEY

I'm so
happy

JUST MARRIED

WHAT THE
NEWLYWEDS CALLED
THEIR FIRST TRIP.

Now arrange the circled letters to form
the surprise answer, as suggested by the
above cartoon.

Print answer here A "  "

JUMBLE®

Unscramble these four Jumbles, one letter
to each square, to form four ordinary words.

WECIT

NIFSI

GUMPSY

DIPSUT

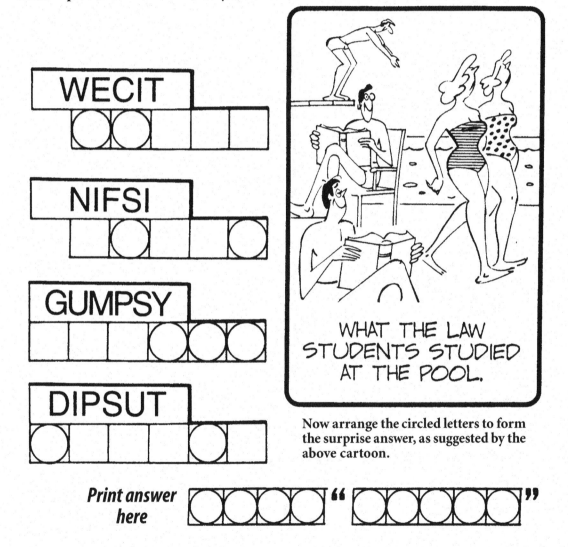

WHAT THE LAW
STUDENTS STUDIED
AT THE POOL.

Now arrange the circled letters to form
the surprise answer, as suggested by the
above cartoon.

Print answer here ◯◯◯◯ " ◯◯◯◯◯ "

JUMBLE®

Unscramble these four Jumbles, one letter to each square, to form four ordinary words.

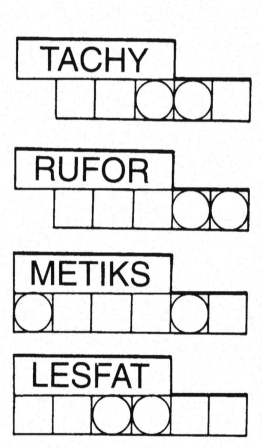

TACHY

RUFOR

METIKS

LESFAT

Mmm--just right _____

HOW THE GEOLOGIST LIKED HIS DRINKS.

Now arrange the circled letters to form the surprise answer, as suggested by the above cartoon.

Print answer here ON

76

JUMBLE®

Unscramble these four Jumbles, one letter to each square, to form four ordinary words.

SABSI

LIXEE

FRYLUR

GAYNIP

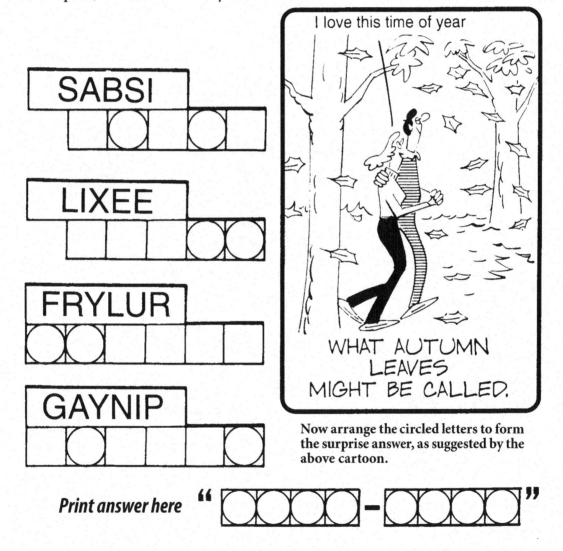

I love this time of year

WHAT AUTUMN LEAVES MIGHT BE CALLED.

Now arrange the circled letters to form the surprise answer, as suggested by the above cartoon.

Print answer here " ⬡⬡⬡⬡ – ⬡⬡⬡⬡ "

JUMBLE®

Unscramble these four Jumbles, one letter
to each square, to form four ordinary words.

VINGE

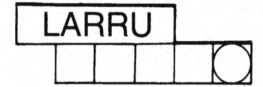

LARRU

UNEEVA

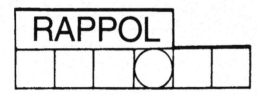

RAPPOL

I believe in an honest day's work

THEY TRUSTED THE
CARPENTER BECAUSE
HE SEEMED ----

Now arrange the circled letters to form
the surprise answer, as suggested by the
above cartoon.

Print answer here   ON
THE "◯◯◯◯◯"

JUMBLE®

Unscramble these four Jumbles, one letter
to each square, to form four ordinary words.

MOIFT

INFEG

TAYFUL

MESSTY

NO SMOKING

Hey--can't you read?

WHEN HE LIT
UP IN A NO
SMOKING AREA HE
LEFT OTHERS ---

Now arrange the circled letters to form
the surprise answer, as suggested by the
above cartoon.

Print answer here

JUMBLE.

Unscramble these four Jumbles, one letter to each square, to form four ordinary words.

MENOG

GWEED

DETHOB

AMLAMM

I bet I can beat you!

You're on!

WHAT THE KIDS DID AT THE PARK.

Now arrange the circled letters to form the surprise answer, as suggested by the above cartoon.

Print answer here THEY " ◯◯◯◯◯◯◯◯ "

JUMBLE®

Unscramble these four Jumbles, one letter
to each square, to form four ordinary words.

RARBI

LAANC

DUBOYE

TALPEA

HOW THEY
FED THE FLAMES
OF LOVE.

Now arrange the circled letters to form
the surprise answer, as suggested by the
above cartoon.

Print answer here " ◯◯◯◯◯◯◯◯ "

JUMBLE®

Unscramble these four Jumbles, one letter to each square, to form four ordinary words.

CIHRB

URUGA

DEBBIA

UMCAUV

It's like a rock!

YOU eat it!

WHAT THEY CALLED THE BAKER WHO SOLD THEM STALE BREAD.

Now arrange the circled letters to form the surprise answer, as suggested by the above cartoon.

Print answer here A ☐☐☐ ☐☐☐☐☐

JUMBLE®

Unscramble these four Jumbles, one letter
to each square, to form four ordinary words.

WYSON

HALTE

DISNAL

DORICH

How many know what this is?

HOW THE
SILHOUETTE
ARTISTS DESCRIBED
THEIR WORK.

Now arrange the circled letters to form
the surprise answer, as suggested by the
above cartoon.

Print answer here BY A ⬡⬡⬡⬡ OF ⬡⬡⬡⬡⬡

JUMBLE®

Unscramble these four Jumbles, one letter
to each square, to form four ordinary words.

NOWDY

MABLY

DYNKIL

ZERBAN

Same old sights

WHAT THEY CALLED
THEIR DAILY
OCEAN STROLL.

Now arrange the circled letters to form
the surprise answer, as suggested by the
above cartoon.

**Print answer
here** THE " ⬡⬡⬡⬡⬡⬡ " ⬡⬡⬡⬡

JUMBLE®

Unscramble these four Jumbles, one letter
to each square, to form four ordinary words.

HOPUC

YURLS

JEDGAG

NOVISI

Did you hear about Mabel?

WHAT THE
ORANGE SQUEEZERS
EXCHANGED.

Now arrange the circled letters to form
the surprise answer, as suggested by the
above cartoon.

**Print answer
here**

JUMBLE®

Unscramble these four Jumbles, one letter
to each square, to form four ordinary words.

VAROS

LYKIS

CORRAN

AREPPA

WHAT THE GOLFERS
THOUGHT THEIR
OUTFITS GAVE THEM.

3-7

Now arrange the circled letters to form
the surprise answer, as suggested by the
above cartoon.

Print answer
here " _____ _____ "

JUMBLE®

Unscramble these four Jumbles, one letter
to each square, to form four ordinary words.

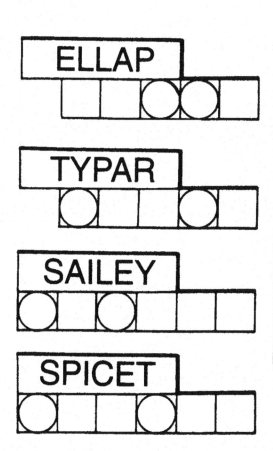

ELLAP

TYPAR

SAILEY

SPICET

Next, get
some shingles

HOW THE ROOFER
TRAINED HIS
APPRENTICE.

Now arrange the circled letters to form
the surprise answer, as suggested by the
above cartoon.

Print answer here

JUMBLE®

Unscramble these four Jumbles, one letter
to each square, to form four ordinary words.

WOGAL

MAGDO

RABLER

PENOLL

Bessie is saving
you work

WHAT THEY
CALLED THE COW
IN THEIR
FRONT YARD.

Now arrange the circled letters to form
the surprise answer, as suggested by the
above cartoon.

*Print answer
here* A ⬭⬭⬭⬭ " ⬭⬭⬭ – ⬭⬭ "

JUMBLE®

Unscramble these four Jumbles, one letter
to each square, to form four ordinary words.

CAPNI

DYPET

ENJUKT

HUHRTS

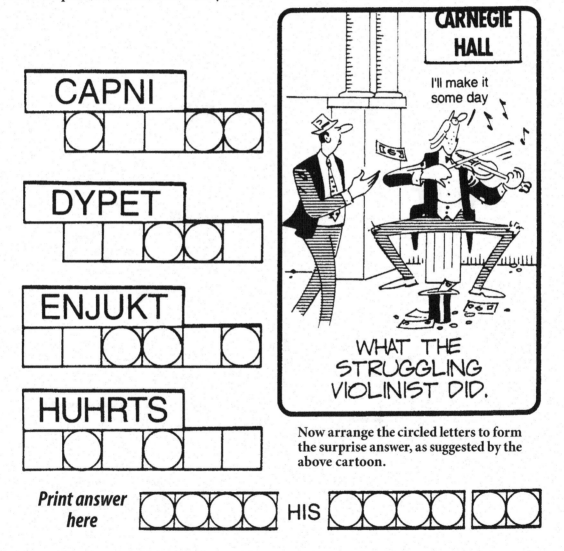

CARNEGIE HALL

I'll make it some day

WHAT THE
STRUGGLING
VIOLINIST DID.

Now arrange the circled letters to form
the surprise answer, as suggested by the
above cartoon.

Print answer here ☐☐☐☐ HIS ☐☐☐☐☐ ☐☐

JUMBLE®

Unscramble these four Jumbles, one letter
to each square, to form four ordinary words.

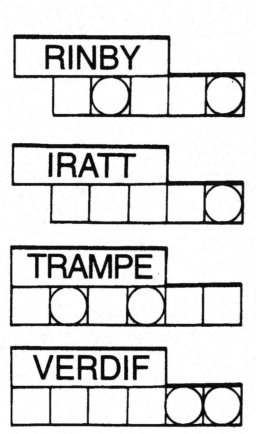

RINBY

IRATT

TRAMPE

VERDIF

THE MINER
STRUCK THIS.

Now arrange the circled letters to form
the surprise answer, as suggested by the
above cartoon.

Print answer here

90

JUMBLE®

Unscramble these four Jumbles, one letter
to each square, to form four ordinary words.

KREJY

GOBEF

TASHAG

PHARCE

WHAT SHE GOT
FROM THE
ELECTRICIAN'S BILL.

Now arrange the circled letters to form
the surprise answer, as suggested by the
above cartoon.

*Print answer
here*

JUMBLE®

Unscramble these four Jumbles, one letter to each square, to form four ordinary words.

ZEFOR

KLABY

DACUDE

QUIROL

Why aren't you working?!

ANOTHER NAME FOR THE SLEEPING BOVINE.

Now arrange the circled letters to form the surprise answer, as suggested by the above cartoon.

Print answer here A ⬡⬡⬡⬡ " ⬡⬡⬡⬡⬡ "

92

JUMBLE®

Unscramble these four Jumbles, one letter to each square, to form four ordinary words.

SWEHL

CAROK

ETTORP

RENACK

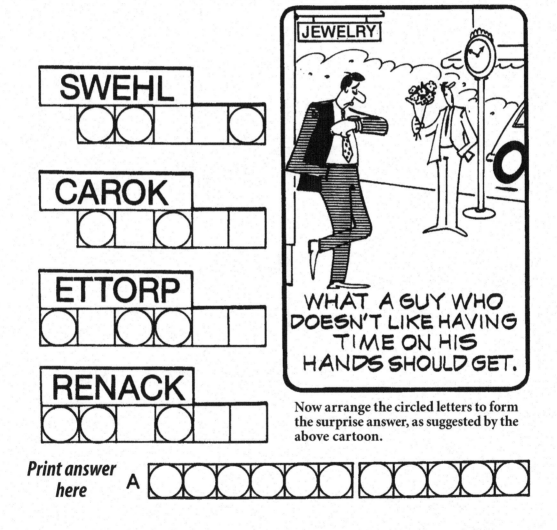

JEWELRY

WHAT A GUY WHO DOESN'T LIKE HAVING TIME ON HIS HANDS SHOULD GET.

Now arrange the circled letters to form the surprise answer, as suggested by the above cartoon.

Print answer here A

93

JUMBLE®

Unscramble these four Jumbles, one letter
to each square, to form four ordinary words.

RYJEK

SERCS

BIMEBI

LEPPUR

WHAT THE
TALKATIVE CUSTOMER
SAID TO THE
BORED BARTENDER.

Now arrange the circled letters to form
the surprise answer, as suggested by the
above cartoon.

*Print
answer* PLEASE " ⬡⬡⬡⬡ " WITH ⬡⬡
here

JUMBLE®

Unscramble these four Jumbles, one letter
to each square, to form four ordinary words.

GYTAN

MAGDO

TADEEB

ZARBLE

4-2

WHAT THE DOCTOR
CHARGED TO FIX UP
THE GUY WHO
INJURED HIS ELBOW
AND KNEE.

Now arrange the circled letters to form
the surprise answer, as suggested by the
above cartoon.

Print answer here AN ◯◯◯ & A ◯◯◯

JUMBLE®

Unscramble these four Jumbles, one letter
to each square, to form four ordinary words.

SINOE

SPEHE

UPDYTE

GANEET

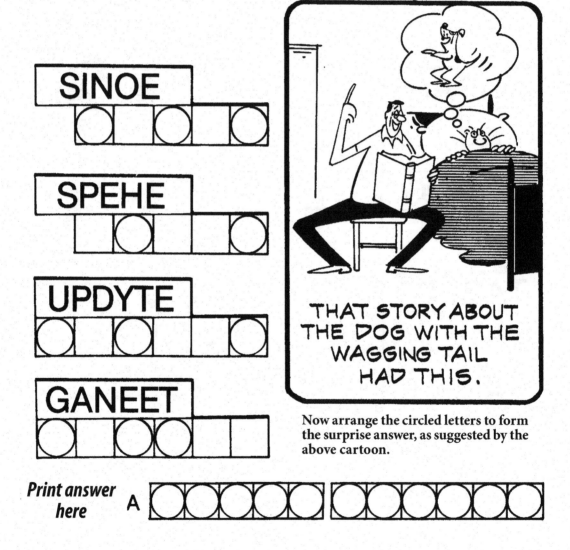

THAT STORY ABOUT
THE DOG WITH THE
WAGGING TAIL
HAD THIS.

Now arrange the circled letters to form
the surprise answer, as suggested by the
above cartoon.

*Print answer
here*   A

JUMBLE®

Unscramble these four Jumbles, one letter to each square, to form four ordinary words.

OCCIL

TOAQU

WULTOA

RYLURF

O Sole mio

THE GONDOLIER MAY BE SERENADING YOU, BUT HE'S READY FOR THIS.

Now arrange the circled letters to form the surprise answer, as suggested by the above cartoon.

Print answer here ◯ " ◯◯◯ "

97

JUMBLE®

Unscramble these four Jumbles, one letter to each square, to form four ordinary words.

TAIMY

SARBS

ENSTEW

DELPOW

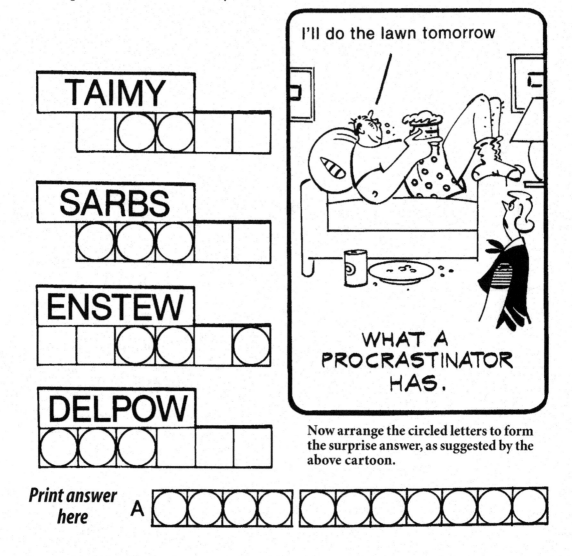

I'll do the lawn tomorrow

WHAT A PROCRASTINATOR HAS.

Now arrange the circled letters to form the surprise answer, as suggested by the above cartoon.

Print answer here A

98

JUMBLE®

Unscramble these four Jumbles, one letter
to each square, to form four ordinary words.

PLEEX

CLEAB

FISHET

RAZDAH

There's a
hair in
my soup

No
extra
charge

A "GREASY SPOON"
IS A RESTAURANT
WHERE YOU CAN
EAT THIS.

Now arrange the circled letters to form
the surprise answer, as suggested by the
above cartoon.

Print answer here

JUMBLE®

Unscramble these four Jumbles, one letter
to each square, to form four ordinary words.

PHOWO

ICHED

MUNCOL

NIXFIG

LANGUAGE USED BY
THOSE PRETENTIOUS
JET-SETTERS.

Now arrange the circled letters to form
the surprise answer, as suggested by the
above cartoon.

Print answer here ◯◯◯◯ — ◯◯◯◯◯

JUMBLE®

Unscramble these four Jumbles, one letter
to each square, to form four ordinary words.

UNMOD

INHEW

HASRIG

TRUFUE

WHAT A SHOTGUN
WEDDING IS A
CASE OF.

Now arrange the circled letters to form
the surprise answer, as suggested by the
above cartoon.

Print answer here ⬭⬭⬭⬭ OR ⬭⬭⬭⬭⬭

JUMBLE®

Unscramble these four Jumbles, one letter to each square, to form four ordinary words.

LYGUL

REELD

ENDTOE

BEWOLB

THAT OIL TYCOON SURE WAS THIS!

Now arrange the circled letters to form the surprise answer, as suggested by the above cartoon.

Print answer here " ⬚⬚⬚⬚⬚ " – ⬚⬚ – ⬚⬚

JUMBLE®

Unscramble these four Jumbles, one letter
to each square, to form four ordinary words.

KYWAG

LEETA

CLIOCA

MABGIT

WHAT YOU MIGHT
FIND PLENTY OF IN A
BURNED-OUT
POST OFFICE.

Now arrange the circled letters to form
the surprise answer, as suggested by the
above cartoon.

Print answer here

103

JUMBLE®

Unscramble these four Jumbles, one letter
to each square, to form four ordinary words.

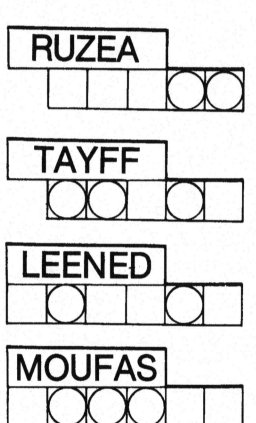

RUZEA

TAYFF

LEENED

MOUFAS

WHAT THE LAZY
BUTCHER WAS.

Now arrange the circled letters to form
the surprise answer, as suggested by the
above cartoon.

*Print answer
here*   A

JUMBLE®

Unscramble these four Jumbles, one letter
to each square, to form four ordinary words.

HIGEW

ROWEB

DEHEAB

LARCOR

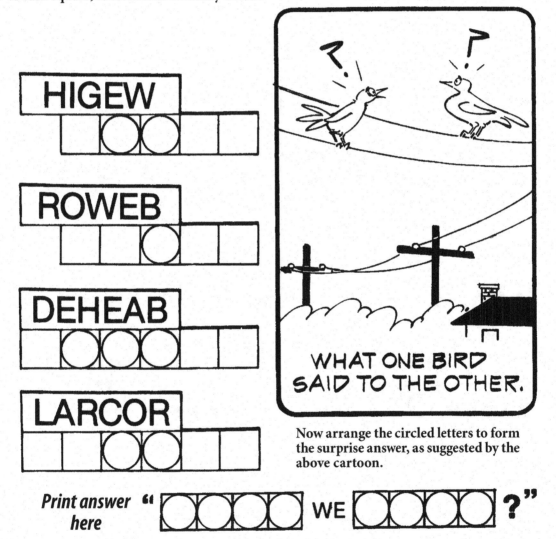

WHAT ONE BIRD
SAID TO THE OTHER.

Now arrange the circled letters to form
the surprise answer, as suggested by the
above cartoon.

*Print answer
here* " ☐☐☐☐☐ WE ☐☐☐☐ ?"

JUMBLE®

Unscramble these four Jumbles, one letter
to each square, to form four ordinary words.

DUSEE

MYJUP

MOHFAT

RANCOY

Mine!

WHAT THE
AGGRESSIVE
FELINE WAS.

Now arrange the circled letters to form
the surprise answer, as suggested by the
above cartoon.

Print answer here A " ⬡⬡⬡⬡⬡ " ⬡⬡⬡

JUMBLE®

Unscramble these four Jumbles, one letter
to each square, to form four ordinary words.

ESTUG

KIHCT

CERTIM

USDABE

I can see fine now,
thanks to you

HOW THE EYE
DOCTOR MIGHT
MAKE YOUR LIFE.

Now arrange the circled letters to form
the surprise answer, as suggested by the
above cartoon.

Print
answer A " ⬡⬡⬡⬡⬡ " ⬡⬡⬡⬡⬡⬡
here

JUMBLE®

Unscramble these four Jumbles, one letter to each square, to form four ordinary words.

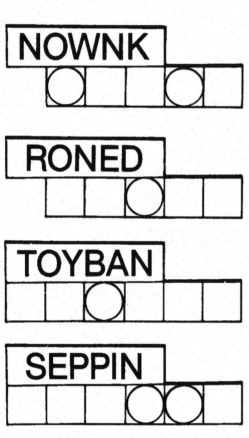

NOWNK

RONED

TOYBAN

SEPPIN

WHAT SKIERS GET INSTEAD OF ATHLETE'S FOOT.

Now arrange the circled letters to form the surprise answer, as suggested by the above cartoon.

Print answer here  " "

JUMBLE®

Unscramble these four Jumbles, one letter
to each square, to form four ordinary words.

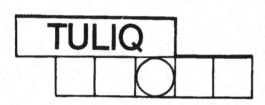

TULIQ

ARZYC

GALEEB

NENFLE

COMING CLOSER—
COULD IT BE
"IN RANGE"?

Now arrange the circled letters to form
the surprise answer, as suggested by the
above cartoon.

Print answer here " ⃝⃝⃝⃝⃝⃝⃝ "

JUMBLE®

Unscramble these four Jumbles, one letter
to each square, to form four ordinary words.

WALOG

SIADY

REMMIO

HINSAV

WHAT YOU GET
IF YOU EAT
TOO MUCH.

Now arrange the circled letters to form
the surprise answer, as suggested by the
above cartoon.

Print answer here A "☐☐☐☐☐ ☐☐☐☐"

JUMBLE®

Unscramble these four Jumbles, one letter to each square, to form four ordinary words.

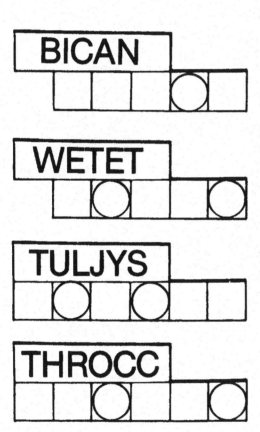

BICAN

WETET

TULJYS

THROCC

CAVIAR
TRUFFLES

No!

3/13

WHAT YOU OFTEN
HAVE TO DO TO
STAY WITHIN
YOUR BUDGET.

Now arrange the circled letters to form the surprise answer, as suggested by the above cartoon.

Print answer here

JUMBLE®

Unscramble these four Jumbles, one letter to each square, to form four ordinary words.

YUMOS

MEERY

CHUNQE

LAMMAM

WHAT THE PHARAOH WHO ATE CRACKERS IN BED WAS.

Now arrange the circled letters to form the surprise answer, as suggested by the above cartoon.

Print answer here A ☐☐☐☐☐☐ ☐☐☐☐☐

JUMBLE®

Unscramble these four Jumbles, one letter
to each square, to form four ordinary words.

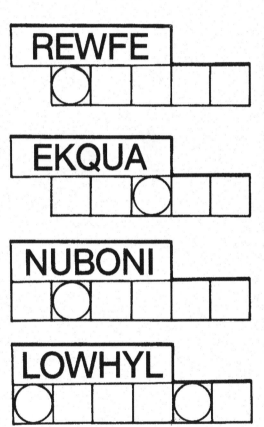

REWFE

EKQUA

NUBONI

LOWHYL

My attorney will
communicate with you!

THIS IS TERRIBLE—
BUT A LETTER
WOULD MAKE
IT LEGAL.

Now arrange the circled letters to form
the surprise answer, as suggested by the
above cartoon.

Print answer here

JUMBLE®

Unscramble these four Jumbles, one letter
to each square, to form four ordinary words.

WONGI

ZIRPE

LOSTCY

SUMMUE

WHAT DO YOU
SERVE HERE?

Now arrange the circled letters to form
the surprise answer, as suggested by the
above cartoon.

Print answer here " ◯◯◯◯ TO ◯◯◯◯ "

114

JUMBLE

Unscramble these four Jumbles, one letter
to each square, to form four ordinary words.

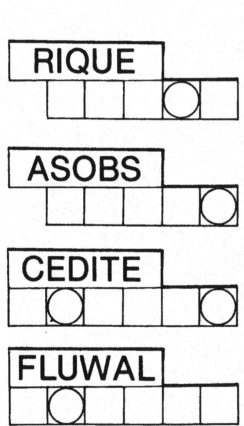

RIQUE

ASOBS

CEDITE

FLUWAL

. . . And in conclusion . . .

MAKE A SPEECH
WITH AN ELABORATE
ENDING.

Now arrange the circled letters to form
the surprise answer, as suggested by the
above cartoon.

Print answer here "  "

JUMBLE®

Unscramble these four Jumbles, one letter
to each square, to form four ordinary words.

YOCEV

GOBUM

TAWNUL

NOXEGY

How nice

THIS ROOM IS
JUST RIGHT FOR
COCKTAILS.

Now arrange the circled letters to form
the surprise answer, as suggested by the
above cartoon.

Print answer here " ◯◯◯◯◯ "

JUMBLE®

Unscramble these four Jumbles, one letter to each square, to form four ordinary words.

RYPOG

LUGEY

NUIJER

RUFIAN

WHERE THE SHORT SPRINTER WAS UNEXPECTEDLY SUCCESSFUL.

Now arrange the circled letters to form the surprise answer, as suggested by the above cartoon.

Print answer here IN THE ⬡⬡⬡⬡⬡ ⬡⬡⬡

JUMBLE®

Unscramble these four Jumbles, one letter
to each square, to form four ordinary words.

YAHND

VERBA

SPITTY

CAPELA

Oh, dear—
I forgot
this one

THERE'S AN EXTRA
LETTER AMID "SHUFFLED"
PAPERS—*MAYBE!*

Now arrange the circled letters to form
the surprise answer, as suggested by the
above cartoon.

Print answer here " ☐☐☐ – ☐ – ☐☐☐ "

JUMBLE®

Unscramble these four Jumbles, one letter
to each square, to form four ordinary words.

HYSYL

TOCET

RAYPER

HEERIT

JUSTICE OF THE PEACE

WHAT USUALLY HAPPENS
WHEN PEOPLE MARRY
IN HASTE?

Now arrange the circled letters to form
the surprise answer, as suggested by the
above cartoon.

Print answer here ☐☐☐☐☐ ☐☐☐☐☐

119

JUMBLE®

Unscramble these four Jumbles, one letter to each square, to form four ordinary words.

GEFOB

BIMOL

YOANNE

ROQUIL

WHAT THE DENTIST'S FAVORITE DISH WAS.

Now arrange the circled letters to form the surprise answer, as suggested by the above cartoon.

Print answer here " ⬭⬭⬭⬭⬭⬭⬭ "

JUMBLE®

Unscramble these four Jumbles, one letter
to each square, to form four ordinary words.

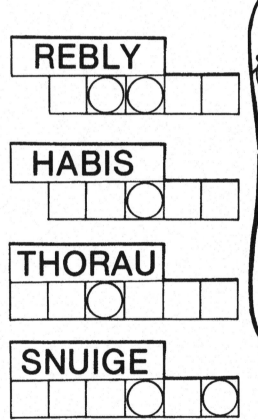

REBLY

HABIS

THORAU

SNUIGE

Here! It's
all yours!

THE TAX PEOPLE
TAKE WHAT
THEY HAVE!

Now arrange the circled letters to form
the surprise answer, as suggested by the
above cartoon.

Print answer here " ☐☐☐ – ☐☐☐ "

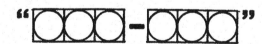

121

JUMBLE®

Unscramble these four Jumbles, one letter
to each square, to form four ordinary words.

GUBYL

SYRTT

LOUBED

MALFEE

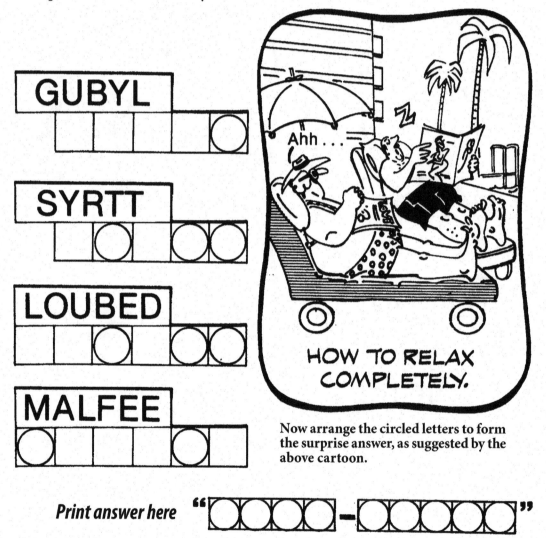

Ahh . . .

**HOW TO RELAX
COMPLETELY.**

Now arrange the circled letters to form
the surprise answer, as suggested by the
above cartoon.

Print answer here " ⬡⬡⬡⬡⬡ – ⬡⬡⬡⬡⬡ "

JUMBLE®

Unscramble these four Jumbles, one letter
to each square, to form four ordinary words.

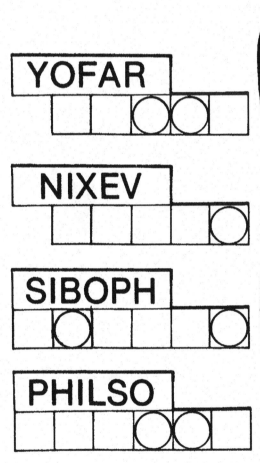

YOFAR

NIXEV

SIBOPH

PHILSO

YES—IT **COULD**
"DISPEL" PAIN, SIR!

Now arrange the circled letters to form
the surprise answer, as suggested by the
above cartoon.

Print answer here "  "

JUMBLE®

Unscramble these four Jumbles, one letter to each square, to form four ordinary words.

KLULS

BIBAR

GANNIA

LEMPOC

Looks like a fighter!

PETS

WOOF WOOF!

A DOG THAT SOUNDS LIKE A BOXER.

Now arrange the circled letters to form the surprise answer, as suggested by the above cartoon.

Print answer here ◯ ◯◯◯

JUMBLE®

Unscramble these four Jumbles, one letter to each square, to form four ordinary words.

ROFAL

POCUR

TOPITE

NORREC

I say ours is the best!

WHAT AN AGGRESSIVE BUSINESSMAN STOUTLY PUSHED FORWARD.

Now arrange the circled letters to form the surprise answer, as suggested by the above cartoon.

Print answer here HIS "◯◯◯◯◯◯◯◯◯◯◯◯"

JUMBLE®

Unscramble these four Jumbles, one letter
to each square, to form four ordinary words.

RYKUM

LEEBI

ENLOOD

DORINO

Tall and willowy

THE EGOTIST'S FAVORITE FIGURE.

Now arrange the circled letters to form
the surprise answer, as suggested by the
above cartoon.

Print answer here ⬡⬡⬡⬡⬡⬡ ⬡⬡⬡

JUMBLE®

Unscramble these four Jumbles, one letter
to each square, to form four ordinary words.

EGBIE

POVER

MYCALL

MEEFAL

It's the
last of
the evening
. . . will you
join me?

A DANCE TO
WIND UP WITH.

Now arrange the circled letters to form
the surprise answer, as suggested by the
above cartoon.

Print answer here **THE**

JUMBLE®

Unscramble these four Jumbles, one letter
to each square, to form four ordinary words.

FEWAR

TEABA

YAMFIL

GINDHI

Sell sell sell

WHAT SOME INVESTORS
DO WHEN THEY
EXPECT THE MARKET
TO GO DOWN.

Now arrange the circled letters to form
the surprise answer, as suggested by the
above cartoon.

Print answer here " ⬠⬠⬠⬠ " ⬠⬠⬠⬠ **IT**

JUMBLE®

Unscramble these four Jumbles, one letter
to each square, to form four ordinary words.

DUTOO

THOLC

ADUMAR

ENCLAG

A NOTE OF HARMONY
IN MOST HOUSEHOLDS.

Now arrange the circled letters to form
the surprise answer, as suggested by the
above cartoon.

Print answer here " ⬡⬡⬡⬡⬡ "

JUMBLE®

Unscramble these four Jumbles, one letter
to each square, to form four ordinary words.

GERMS

THERE IS LITTLE TO
SEE THROUGH IT.

NACEP

CREMY

BUTSOE

KENVIO

Now arrange the circled letters to form
the surprise answer, as suggested by the
above cartoon.

Print answer here **A**

JUMBLE®

Unscramble these four Jumbles, one letter to each square, to form four ordinary words.

TRIGE

DUTIA

KURBEE

HOARIM

Cures rheumatism, eyestrain, toothache, housemaid's knee . . .

DOC'S CURE ALL

4-11

WHAT THE MEDICINE MAN HAD TROUBLE SELLING.

Now arrange the circled letters to form the surprise answer, as suggested by the above cartoon.

Print answer here

A ☐☐☐☐ ON THE ☐☐☐☐☐☐☐

JUMBLE®

Unscramble these four Jumbles, one letter
to each square, to form four ordinary words.

SNABI

THIRM

SINOUF

UPDELD

OLD CLOTHING MADE
FROM LETTERS.

Now arrange the circled letters to form
the surprise answer, as suggested by the
above cartoon.

Print answer here **A** ◯◯◯◯ **OF** ◯◯◯◯

JUMBLE.

Unscramble these four Jumbles, one letter to each square, to form four ordinary words.

RITTA

KALOC

NAMLEE

TOLBEG

You're handsome AND intelligent

YOU NEED A COMBINATION OF *TACT* AND *ART* TO DO THIS SUCCESSFULLY.

Now arrange the circled letters to form the surprise answer, as suggested by the above cartoon.

Print answer here

JUMBLE®

Unscramble these four Jumbles, one letter
to each square, to form four ordinary words.

WAULF

ORFYT

FORTIP

THIMER

Oh,
honey!

$100

4-7

WHAT COLD CASH OFTEN
MAKES PEOPLE DO.

Now arrange the circled letters to form
the surprise answer, as suggested by the
above cartoon.

Print answer here

JUMBLE®

Unscramble these four Jumbles, one letter
to each square, to form four ordinary words.

TACUE

SAYID

REWEPT

SCUMEL

WHAT HAPPENED TO
THE BAKED GOODS?

Now arrange the circled letters to form
the surprise answer, as suggested by the
above cartoon.

*Print
answer
here*   **THEY WERE "◯◯◯-◯◯◯◯◯"**

JUMBLE®

Unscramble these four Jumbles, one letter
to each square, to form four ordinary words.

ENVOW

CASIB

TINADY

PERMET

WHAT THE MAN
WHO WORE TWO SUITS
TO A MASQUERADE
PARTY WENT AS.

Now arrange the circled letters to form
the surprise answer, as suggested by the
above cartoon.

Print answer here

JUMBLE®

Unscramble these four Jumbles, one letter
to each square, to form four ordinary words.

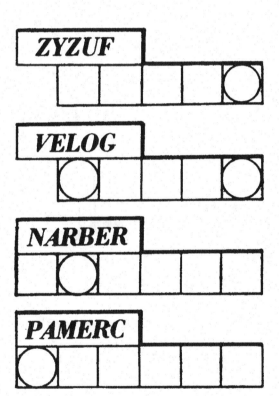

ZYZUF

VELOG

NARBER

PAMERC

Maybe later

HOW TO HANDLE
A HUMAN BEAST.

Now arrange the circled letters to form
the surprise answer, as suggested by the
above cartoon.

Print answer here **BE** ⬡⬡⬡⬡⬡

JUMBLE®

Unscramble these four Jumbles, one letter
to each square, to form four ordinary words.

NAJOB

FREVE

YELLIK

TIVNAY

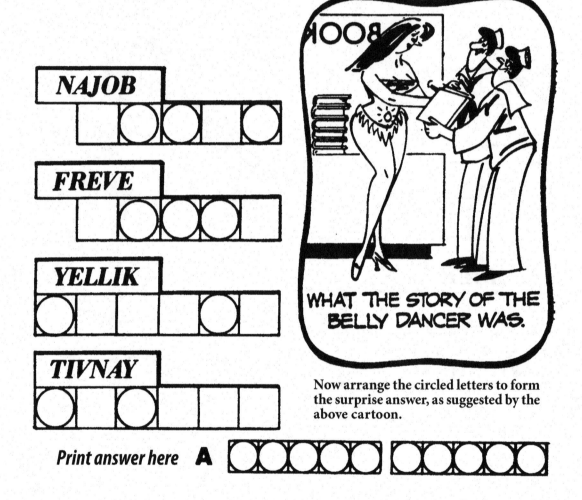

WHAT THE STORY OF THE
BELLY DANCER WAS.

Now arrange the circled letters to form
the surprise answer, as suggested by the
above cartoon.

Print answer here **A**

JUMBLE®

Unscramble these four Jumbles, one letter
to each square, to form four ordinary words.

CEEPA

VORSA

SEPORC

ROAMON

THIS CAN MAKE A
HASH OF MARRIAGE.

Now arrange the circled letters to form
the surprise answer, as suggested by the
above cartoon.

Print answer here

JUMBLE®

Unscramble these four Jumbles, one letter
to each square, to form four ordinary words.

TIFAH

KALCH

YARFER

DESMOT

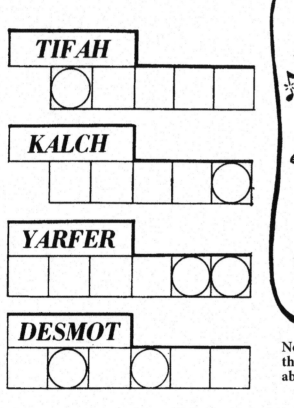

Oh, dry up!

HOW THE UNHAPPY
LOCKSMITH SANG.

Now arrange the circled letters to form
the surprise answer, as suggested by the
above cartoon.

Print answer here ◯◯◯ – ◯◯◯

JUMBLE®

Unscramble these four Jumbles, one letter
to each square, to form four ordinary words.

KOAWE

URRYC

TULTER

RUFIAN

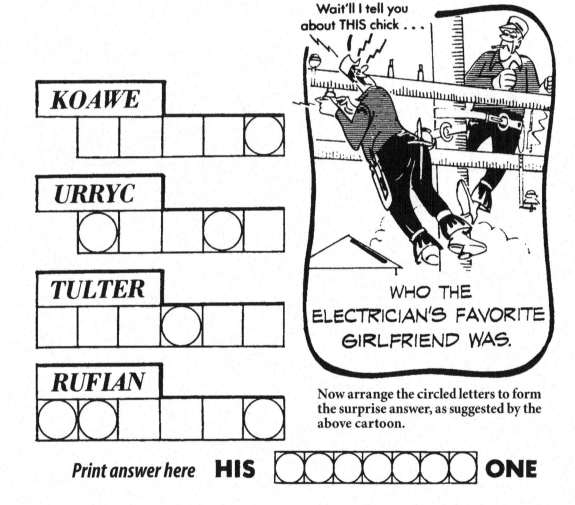

Wait'll I tell you
about THIS chick . . .

WHO THE
ELECTRICIAN'S FAVORITE
GIRLFRIEND WAS.

Now arrange the circled letters to form
the surprise answer, as suggested by the
above cartoon.

Print answer here **HIS** ⬡⬡⬡⬡⬡⬡⬡ **ONE**

JUMBLE ®

Unscramble these four Jumbles, one letter to each square, to form four ordinary words.

WEELJ

YUHRR

GROINI

SLOMBY

Back home in . . .

A COVER-UP IN INDIANA.

Now arrange the circled letters to form the surprise answer, as suggested by the above cartoon.

Print answer here " ◯◯◯◯◯◯◯◯◯ "

142

JUMBLE

Unscramble these four Jumbles, one letter to each square, to form four ordinary words.

EGBOY

HOYNE

SOUREA

RUBETT

WHAT THEY WERE IN THE NURSERY.

Now arrange the circled letters to form the surprise answer, as suggested by the above cartoon.

Print answer here

☐☐☐☐☐☐ **AS** ☐☐☐☐☐

JUMBLE®

Unscramble these four Jumbles, one letter
to each square, to form four ordinary words.

GUCOH

TURSY

TALLEB

RUFTUE

WHAT THE CRAZY
ROWER WHO FELL
OUT OF HIS RACING
BOAT WAS.

Now arrange the circled letters to form
the surprise answer, as suggested by the
above cartoon.

Print answer here ◯◯◯ **OF HIS** ◯◯◯◯◯

JUMBLE®

Unscramble these four Jumbles, one letter
to each square, to form four ordinary words.

PEALL

SELBS

REPOOC

PANPHE

HOW THE BANANA
TYCOON LOST
A LAWSUIT.

Now arrange the circled letters to form
the surprise answer, as suggested by the
above cartoon.

Print answer here ◯◯ **A** ◯◯◯◯

JUMBLE®

Unscramble these four Jumbles, one letter
to each square, to form four ordinary words.

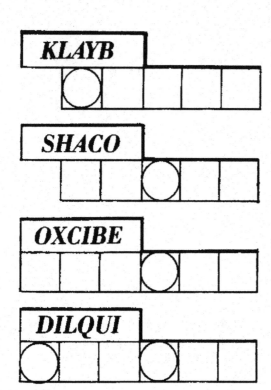

KLAYB

SHACO

OXCIBE

DILQUI

THIS MIGHT BE AN
ELECTRIC LIGHT PLANT.

Now arrange the circled letters to form
the surprise answer, as suggested by the
above cartoon.

Print answer here

146

JUMBLE®

Unscramble these four Jumbles, one letter
to each square, to form four ordinary words.

TULDA

TENIL

RAWSUL

QUALEP

HOW HE
PRODUCED OIL.

Now arrange the circled letters to form
the surprise answer, as suggested by the
above cartoon.

Print answer here

JUMBLE®

Unscramble these four Jumbles, one letter to each square, to form four ordinary words.

SYTUM

NATOE

TOPATE

DRAHLY

Now you've tried them all.

THIS MIGHT BE THE LATEST SHOE MODEL.

Now arrange the circled letters to form the surprise answer, as suggested by the above cartoon.

Print answer here

JUMBLE®

Unscramble these four Jumbles, one letter
to each square, to form four ordinary words.

CNOTH

SOYUL

LEDENE

TARRMY

NO MORE
SEATS

WHERE YOU
MIGHT SIT.

Now arrange the circled letters to form
the surprise answer, as suggested by the
above cartoon.

Print answer here **IN A** ⬡⬡⬡⬡⬡

JUMBLE ®

Unscramble these four Jumbles, one letter to each square, to form four ordinary words.

VELGA

AXORB

ZEMENY

NOOTIL

THE DELICATESSEN MAN'S WIFE SUMMED UP HIS ALIBI IN ONE WORD.

Now arrange the circled letters to form the surprise answer, as suggested by the above cartoon.

Print answer here " O O O O O O O ! "

150

JUMBLE®

Unscramble these four Jumbles, one letter to each square, to form four ordinary words.

TARAP

NAKEW

YUCLOD

MAYGIB

This is unauthorized!

THIS KIND OF STRIKE MIGHT CAUSE TROUBLE AT THE ZOO.

Now arrange the circled letters to form the surprise answer, as suggested by the above cartoon.

Print answer here

JUMBLE®

Unscramble these four Jumbles, one letter
to each square, to form four ordinary words.

CAPNI

GAMLE

LURSEY

ANSTUE

HOW THE CLOWN IN
THE GEOLOGY CLASS
DEFINED "BEDROCK."

Now arrange the circled letters to form
the surprise answer, as suggested by the
above cartoon.

Print
answer
here "⬡⬡⬡⬡⬡ TO ⬡⬡⬡⬡⬡ BY "

JUMBLE®

Unscramble these four Jumbles, one letter
to each square, to form four ordinary words.

YARIF

DUHMI

NOPETT

CONTOY

WHAT A GUY WHO
GOT COLD FEET BEFORE
THE WEDDING DID.

Now arrange the circled letters to form
the surprise answer, as suggested by the
above cartoon.

Print answer here ◯◯◯◯◯◯◯◯◯ **IT**

153

JUMBLE®

Unscramble these four Jumbles, one letter
to each square, to form four ordinary words.

ZENOO

VALIT

MEEPID

COYPIL

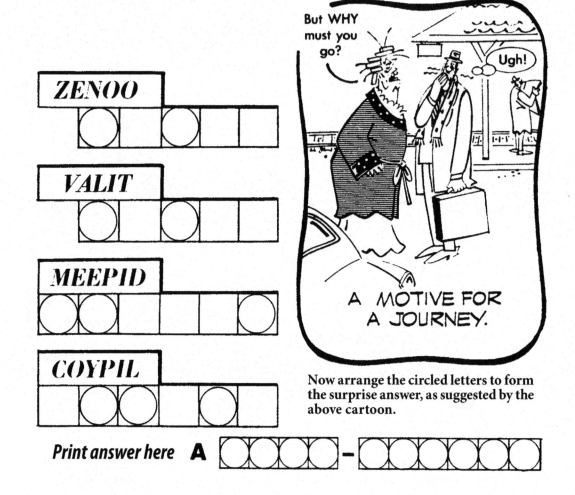

But WHY
must you
go?

Ugh!

A MOTIVE FOR
A JOURNEY.

Now arrange the circled letters to form
the surprise answer, as suggested by the
above cartoon.

Print answer here **A** ◯◯◯◯◯ — ◯◯◯◯◯◯◯

JUMBLE®

Unscramble these four Jumbles, one letter
to each square, to form four ordinary words.

YAHND

RADIC

EMORCH

YEUFLE

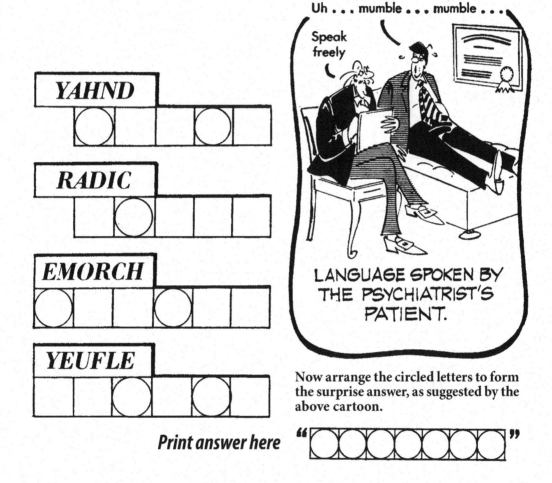

Uh . . . mumble . . . mumble . . .

Speak freely

LANGUAGE SPOKEN BY
THE PSYCHIATRIST'S
PATIENT.

Now arrange the circled letters to form
the surprise answer, as suggested by the
above cartoon.

Print answer here " ◯◯◯◯◯◯◯◯ "

JUMBLE®

Unscramble these four Jumbles, one letter
to each square, to form four ordinary words.

URRJO

CUIMS

WISDON

SUTTOM

Look . . .
guess what . . .

Oh,
shut
up!

2-10

GOSSIP CAN BE
A PAIN WHEN
IT'S THIS.

Now arrange the circled letters to form
the surprise answer, as suggested by the
above cartoon.

Print answer here ◯◯◯◯◯ - ◯◯◯◯◯

JUMBLE®

Unscramble these four Jumbles, one letter to each square, to form four ordinary words.

LAUVE

GUDOH

CREELY

GURTIA

WHAT A CRAVAT TYCOON MIGHT EXPECT PLENTY OF FROM THE NEW WIDE STYLES.

Now arrange the circled letters to form the surprise answer, as suggested by the above cartoon.

Print answer here

JUMBLE®

Unscramble these four Jumbles, one letter
to each square, to form four ordinary words.

NOOLC

PEGRI

GLOUEY

ZARLID

WORDS THAT TELL
YOU THERE MIGHT BE
SOMETHING UNLAWFUL
ABOUT THIS SICK BIRD.

Now arrange the circled letters to form
the surprise answer, as suggested by the
above cartoon.

Print answer here "⬡⬡⬡ ⬡⬡⬡⬡⬡"

JUMBLE.

Unscramble these four Jumbles, one letter
to each square, to form four ordinary words.

DANAP

YIKTT

DONBEY

RYSLIG

WHAT THE PIG
SAID AS THE SUN
GREW HOTTER.

2-6

Now arrange the circled letters to form
the surprise answer, as suggested by the
above cartoon.

Print answer here **I'M** ⬭⬭⬭⬭⬭'

JUMBLE®

Unscramble these four Jumbles, one letter
to each square, to form four ordinary words.

MYNAL

YEJON

DISTEW

ORISEE

WHEN MOTHER SAW
THE BATHROOM SHE
SAID THIS.

Now arrange the circled letters to form
the surprise answer, as suggested by the
above cartoon.

Print answer here "⬡⬡⬡⬡⬡⬡ ⬡⬡⬡⬡!"

JUMBLE®

Unscramble these four Jumbles, one letter
to each square, to form four ordinary words.

BIATH

LUFTO

URAUBE

MAMBEL

THIS MIGHT BE *THERE* IN OUTER SPACE!

Now arrange the circled letters to form
the surprise answer, as suggested by the
above cartoon.

Print answer here

JUMBLE®

Unscramble these four Jumbles, one letter
to each square, to form four ordinary words.

BOREP

GANOW

DAJEGG

RUBENK

How come you're draggin'?

HOW YOU FEEL AFTER
A BIG WEEKEND.

Now arrange the circled letters to form
the surprise answer, as suggested by the
above cartoon.

Print answer here

JUMBLE®
Gold

Challenger
Puzzles

JUMBLE®

Unscramble these six Jumbles, one letter to each square, to form six ordinary words.

CRIFEE

FONLUD

FRETAL

INECCS

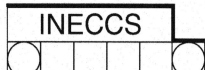

LIMSIE

DEOXUT

Be careful! You're running too close to the edge.

We don't have views like this when we jog at home.

WHEN THEY JOGGED ALONG THE RIM OF THE CANYON, THEY NEEDED TO ---

Now arrange the circled letters to form the surprise answer, as suggested by the above cartoon.

Print answer here

JUMBLE.

Unscramble these six Jumbles, one letter to each square, to form six ordinary words.

PRINTU

KESCIN

FACETF

HNARSK

SPOIGS

PYNEHH

Wow! No one can reach him!

I'm so glad he plays here.

BULLS 23

EVERYONE LOVED WATCHING MICHAEL JORDAN PLAY AT THE ---

Now arrange the circled letters to form the surprise answer, as suggested by the above cartoon.

Print answer here

165

JUMBLE®

Unscramble these six Jumbles, one letter to each square, to form six ordinary words.

GRAHET

VIERRD

LERLON

SDWERH

LAIGEO

MARYEC

AFTER THE KIDS GAVE THEIR MOM HER MOTHER'S DAY PRESENTS, SHE ----

Now arrange the circled letters to form the surprise answer, as suggested by the above cartoon.

Print answer here

166

JUMBLE®

Unscramble these six Jumbles, one letter to each square, to form six ordinary words.

TIRBET

CRINUH

HUCBER

SAFOIC

SUEDOX

MISTAG

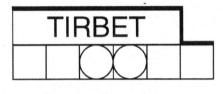

Put that TV down. Then stand there with your arms raised. After that, put your arms behind your back and turn around. I'm going to walk over there to handcuff you. Then, I'll read you your rights...

BEFORE THE COP WAS DONE ARRESTING HIM, THE SUSPECT WAS READY TO ---

Now arrange the circled letters to form the surprise answer, as suggested by the above cartoon.

Print answer here

JUMBLE®

Unscramble these six Jumbles, one letter to each square, to form six ordinary words.

MIMEUD

UDSLOH

RAPLIS

SOMTAC

RAYNEL

TOYNAB

How was your first day working from home?

It was OK, I guess. I didn't realize how much I liked having co-workers around. It's going to take some getting used to.

SHE QUIT HER OFFICE JOB TO START HER OWN BUSINESS FROM HOME, BUT SHE ----

Now arrange the circled letters to form the surprise answer, as suggested by the above cartoon.

Print answer here

JUMBLE®

Unscramble these six Jumbles, one letter to each square, to form six ordinary words.

CASIOF

RIDAHO

TWORGH

VEWLET

SUYMAL

DETSOM

I can't seem to keep the pounds off. I've started having double burgers instead of triples.

What if you tried even smaller portions?

HE STRUGGLED TO LOSE WEIGHT BECAUSE HE ALWAYS HAD – – – –

Now arrange the circled letters to form the surprise answer, as suggested by the above cartoon.

Print answer here

" ⬡⬡⬡⬡⬡ " ⬡⬡⬡ ⬡⬡⬡⬡ ⬡⬡⬡⬡

169

JUMBLE®

Unscramble these six Jumbles, one letter to each square, to form six ordinary words.

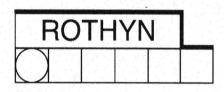

ROTHYN

CTEEND

CINCES

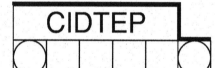

CIDTEP

TARULI

MOLSAN

We're surrounded. This is too much. This was a bad idea.

What do we do, General?

IF YOU COULD ASK GEN. GEORGE ARMSTRONG CUSTER ABOUT HIS LAST BATTLE, HE'D SAY HE ----

Now arrange the circled letters to form the surprise answer, as suggested by the above cartoon.

Print answer here

JUMBLE®

Unscramble these six Jumbles, one letter
to each square, to form six ordinary words.

VAHENE

SEGTAK

CRUNIH

TASYAR

TEYMSS

DUNCIT

I'm not picking
up that brat's
crayons. Do you
even know what
you want yet?
Hurry up. I've got
other tables.

That does it!
He's fired.

Hey! What
did you say?
Where's your
manager?

I'm
scared.

GETTING FIRED FOR
BEING A RUDE AND
OBNOXIOUS WAITER ----

Now arrange the circled letters to form
the surprise answer, as suggested by the
above cartoon.

Print answer here

JUMBLE®

Unscramble these six Jumbles, one letter
to each square, to form six ordinary words.

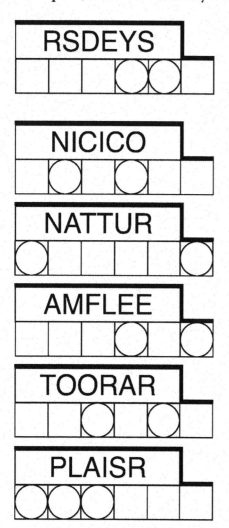

RSDEYS

NICICO

NATTUR

AMFLEE

TOORAR

PLAISR

This is a waste of time. We'll have to watch a DVD again.

As long as it's not "2001" again.

WHAT THE ASTRONAUTS
WISHED THEY HAD FOR
WATCHING TV IN ORBIT.

Now arrange the circled letters to form
the surprise answer, as suggested by the
above cartoon.

Print answer here

JUMBLE®

Unscramble these six Jumbles, one letter to each square, to form six ordinary words.

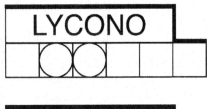

LYCONO

WCYOOB

GVOEAY

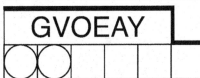

EFBTUF

HLPTIG

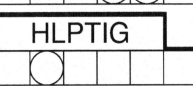

OYTRRA

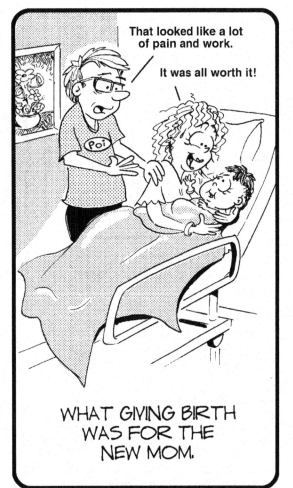

That looked like a lot of pain and work.

It was all worth it!

WHAT GIVING BIRTH WAS FOR THE NEW MOM.

Now arrange the circled letters to form the surprise answer, as suggested by the above cartoon.

Print answer here

A

Unscramble these six Jumbles, one letter
to each square, to form six ordinary words.

THEIRZ

HEETES

KRODEF

TAUMUN

NAGUMM

MOARRY

START

You're all set.
Here's your
number

2017

WHAT HE GOT
WHEN HE PAID TO
ENTER THE MARATHON.

Now arrange the circled letters to form
the surprise answer, as suggested by the
above cartoon.

Print answer here

A " ☐☐☐ " ☐☐☐ ☐☐☐ ☐☐☐☐☐

JUMBLE®

Unscramble these six Jumbles, one letter
to each square, to form six ordinary words.

TALUCA

TRIVUE

TISSIN

HYDING

HYLLOW

MINGOH

We could
use new drapes

Not this
year

1/30

KEEPING YOUR
SPENDING UNDER
CONTROL OFTEN
MEANS THIS.

Now arrange the circled letters to form
the surprise answer, as suggested by the
above cartoon.

Print answer here

JUMBLE®

Unscramble these six Jumbles, one letter to each square, to form six ordinary words.

SMIREY

RILOAS

ROGERF

WALLOH

YORPET

GININN

How was your date last night?

None of your business

WHAT THE FITNESS INSTRUCTOR TURNED INTO.

Now arrange the circled letters to form the surprise answer, as suggested by the above cartoon.

Print answer here

A " ⬡⬡⬡⬡⬡⬡⬡⬡ " ⬡⬡⬡⬡⬡⬡⬡

JUMBLE®

Unscramble these six Jumbles, one letter to each square, to form six ordinary words.

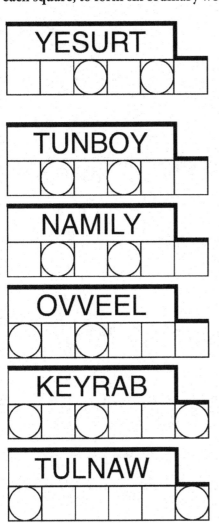

YESURT

TUNBOY

NAMILY

OVVEEL

KEYRAB

TULNAW

Maybe we should advertise

The phones aren't ringing

THE NOVICE BOOKIE SUFFERED TOUGH TIMES BECAUSE HE DIDN'T ---

Now arrange the circled letters to form the surprise answer, as suggested by the above cartoon.

Print answer here

JUMBLE®

Unscramble these six Jumbles, one letter to each square, to form six ordinary words.

NIXFIG

VALMER

NICCES

PANNEM

DULCED

RELAFT

There's no comparison

WHERE AIRLINE AND FIGHTER PILOTS END UP.

Now arrange the circled letters to form the surprise answer, as suggested by the above cartoon.

Print answer here

ON ⟨ ⟩⟨ ⟩⟨ ⟩⟨ ⟩⟨ ⟩⟨ ⟩⟨ ⟩⟨ ⟩ " ⟨ ⟩⟨ ⟩⟨ ⟩⟨ ⟩⟨ ⟩ "

JUMBLE®

Unscramble these six Jumbles, one letter to each square, to form six ordinary words.

WARMOR

GANNIA

SINVIO

NOTINE

BOILAN

LOUGEY

He's busy
building his
house

NATURALLY,
A BEAVER HAS A ---

Now arrange the circled letters to form the surprise answer, as suggested by the above cartoon.

Print answer here

" ◯◯◯◯◯◯◯ " ◯◯◯◯◯◯◯◯

JUMBLE®

Unscramble these six Jumbles, one letter to each square, to form six ordinary words.

FORFET

THROBE

GARAVE

FLAWLU

YARQUR

MAPCEN

It sure is a nasty day

It's good for business

TAXI I500

THE TAXI DRIVER SAID THE RAINY DAY WAS ---

Now arrange the circled letters to form the surprise answer, as suggested by the above cartoon.

Print answer here

" ⃝⃝⃝⃝ " ⃝⃝⃝⃝⃝⃝⃝⃝

JUMBLE®

Unscramble these six Jumbles, one letter to each square, to form six ordinary words.

HINEAL

SHEERY

NERKUB

THROME

AMOWED

TANEBE

You wouldn't think he had a dime

WHY THE OIL BARON DIDN'T SHOW HIS WEALTH.

Now arrange the circled letters to form the surprise answer, as suggested by the above cartoon.

Print answer here

IT

JUMBLE®

Unscramble these six Jumbles, one letter to each square, to form six ordinary words.

COBUNE

RASTUX

EXPLUD

YAMIDD

PHAIMS

COREEN

HE REFUSED TO VISIT THE NUDIST CAMP BECAUSE HE WAS ---

Now arrange the circled letters to form the surprise answer, as suggested by the above cartoon.

Print answer here

JUMBLE®

Unscramble these six Jumbles, one letter to each square, to form six ordinary words.

FUPULC

AUSANE

CERTIM

TIMLEG

QUINAT

BRAKEM

After you, my dear

Thank you, sweetheart

WHEN THE COUPLE RECONCILED, THEY SAID THE MARRIAGE COUNSELOR WAS A ---

Now arrange the circled letters to form the surprise answer, as suggested by the above cartoon.

Print answer here

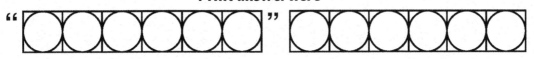

" ◯◯◯◯◯◯ " ◯◯◯◯◯◯

Answers

1. **Jumbles:** ABATE POUCH DRESSY BOXING
Answer: When the surgeon met himself in a parallel universe, it was a — "PAIR-A-DOCS"

2. **Jumbles:** IRONY MUSHY PERSON SOCKET
Answer: The staircase wasn't going to be finished on schedule because of all the — MISSTEPS

3. **Jumbles:** FOCAL RELIC RESUME PERMIT
Answer: They raised chickens and grew pines on their — "POLE-TREE" FARM

4. **Jumbles:** WHEEL PERKY SOOTHE SONATA
Answer: They would let her open her birthday gifts after everyone — WAS PRESENT

5. **Jumbles:** SOGGY IMPEL OUTLET ABLAZE
Answer: King Kong wanted to play for the Yankees, but he was too large for the — BIG LEAGUES

6. **Jumbles:** VOWEL HUMID ASTRAY CHERUB
Answer: They were selling out of Beatles albums in — RECORD TIME

7. **Jumbles:** RAINY HUSKY ATRIUM HUMBLE
Answer: He told his wife he was going jogging, but he should have done this first — RUN IT BY HER

8. **Jumbles:** ABOVE FLUTE INCOME INDIGO
Answer: When they decided not to pull an April 1 prank on readers, their editor said — NO FOOLING

9. **Jumbles:** OPERA ACUTE DRAFTY SEASON
Answer: When the town started charging to use the park, it was a — "FEE-ASCO"

10. **Jumbles:** RIGOR SKIMP HYBRID BOUNCE
Answer: The psychiatrist began to worry about his business after it started to — SHRINK

11. **Jumbles:** IMAGE ELDER DEPICT INSIST
Answer: When she browsed the Internet, she was — "SITE"-SEEING

12. **Jumbles:** ANNUL DERBY SLUDGE IMPACT
Answer: The scarecrow didn't have a brain, and as a result was — ABSENT-MINDED

13. **Jumbles:** HOUND WIPER TRUDGE AMOEBA
Answer: The archer who thought he was the best in the world was — "ARROW-GANT"

14. **Jumbles:** KAZOO HUTCH STRONG COPPER
Answer: To project sales of record players, they used — PHONO-GRAPHS

15. **Jumbles:** HEDGE TRUNK FAULTY FATHOM
Answer: After the stockbroker got married, he was — OFF THE MARKET

16. **Jumbles:** HANDY FLOSS BROKEN ARCHER
Answer: When he put on his grandfather's hat, he was — FEDORABLE

17. **Jumbles:** ERUPT ABOUT CRUMMY CHUNKY
Answer: The QB's girlfriend broke up with him, but he was going to try to — COURT HER BACK

18. **Jumbles:** POUND AGAIN THROAT IMPORT
Answer: After seeing how snug her dress had become, she was — UPTIGHT

19. **Jumbles:** INPUT WEIGH UPROAR NINETY
Answer: The jogger was happy to find some — RUNNING WATER

20. **Jumbles:** RUGBY STUNG CRUNCH ADVICE
Answer: Yogi's family reunion featured — BEAR HUGS

21. **Jumbles:** CROWN HONEY LONELY KITTEN
Answer: He wanted to wear his favorite pair of golf socks, but he had a — HOLE IN ONE

22. **Jumbles:** NIECE ABATE DENOTE BROKER
Answer: After the rock group trashed their hotel suite, they were — BANNED

23. **Jumbles:** PANTS DIVOT FORAGE MISUSE
Answer: They weren't sure what it would be like sailing in the Mediterranean, so they went — OUT TO "SEE"

24. **Jumbles:** PRESS POISE VORTEX BROKEN
Answer: The salesman knew everything about bicycle wheels and made a great — SPOKES-PERSON

25. **Jumbles:** DAISY HARSH IMPEDE SHRINK
Answer: The husband and wife who owned the funeral home had two cars, — HIS AND HEARSE

26. **Jumbles:** IDIOT SHOVE HERMIT FAÇADE
Answer: The owner of the wig shop was the — HEAD OF HAIR

27. **Jumbles:** FLUID WAFER SNITCH VOYAGE
Answer: A popular event at the waterfowl Olympics was the — SWAN DIVE

28. **Jumbles:** DAISY ALIAS UNTOLD EFFORT
Answer: When she had trouble solving the Jumble, asking her father for help was the — SOLUTION

29. **Jumbles:** ADOPT CLASH DOUBLE FILTHY
Answer: When Shakespeare was a kid, putting on a performance was — CHILD'S PLAY

30. **Jumbles:** LIMIT GOING UNSURE FORMAL
Answer: The ladies lined up to sing karaoke — "SING-GAL" FILE

31. **Jumbles:** SENSE BLURT NEURON LAWFUL
Answer: The out-of-control horse was — UN-STABLE

32. **Jumbles:** BLIMP GIANT SPRUNG REDUCE
Answer: After he won the lottery, King Kong became a — BIG SPENDER

33. **Jumbles:** STRUM COVET SESAME REBUKE
Answer: After bumping into the celebrity on the street, she was — STAR STRUCK

34. **Jumbles:** THINK PIVOT PARLOR EXPOSE
Answer: The mountain climber who reached the peak first was in — TIP-TOP SHAPE

35. **Jumbles:** THEFT SLANT PARLAY MIDDLE
Answer: He wanted to go bowling, but he didn't have — SPARE TIME

36. **Jumbles:** HIKER DECAY KNIGHT MINGLE
Answer: The army general who played in the tennis tournament was — HIGHLY RANKED

37. **Jumbles:** WOUND NOVEL DOOMED SUNKEN
Answer: What snobby birds with big egos do — LOOK DOWN ON US

38. **Jumbles:** SENSE ADAGE LETTER LOCKED
Answer: When it came time to explain the team's defeat, the coach was this — AT A LOSS

39. **Jumbles:** BASIC ALIAS GUILTY AROUND
Answer: The umpire was glad the game was finally over because he was ready to — CALL IT A DAY

40. **Jumbles:** GIVEN WOOZY DEPUTY BALLET
Answer: The movie set in Death Valley had a — LOW BUDGET

41. **Jumbles:** GNARL ICING ARTFUL ENTICE
Answer: When the guitarist auditioned for the band, he was — "FRETTING"

42. **Jumbles:** CAPON LYING UNHOOK INFIRM
Answer: This comes out during a debate — YOUR OPINION

43. **Jumbles:** QUAKE SIEGE BUSILY CANINE
Answer: What the poker player had when the royals joined the game — KINGS AND QUEENS

44. **Jumbles:** SHOWY ELITE PALLID MULISH
Answer: What the traffic reporter said when the police chase tied up the roads — "IT'S A HOLD UP"

45. **Jumbles:** CHIDE YOUTH GARLIC STYMIE
Answer: What he got when his wife bought the designer dress — THE "CREDIT"

46. **Jumbles:** JOLLY VAPOR CRABBY FUTILE
Answer: The very top can be achieved from this — POVERTY

47. **Jumbles:** DELVE THICK BECAME EMBODY
Answer: What the ironworkers did when they built the tower — THEY "BEAMED"

48. **Jumbles:** FATAL AIDED ALPACA SOIREE
Answer: What he did when he was offered a chance to skydive — "LEAPED" AT IT

49. **Jumbles:** BASSO ANKLE BOUNCE STIGMA
Answer: The high roller left the casino with a small fortune because he — LOST A BIG ONE

50. **Jumbles:** LADLE EVENT FINISH BEDECK
Answer: What barbed wire is usually used for — DE-FENCE

51. **Jumbles:** HAVEN ELEGY HANDLE MALICE
Answer: What the apprentice did for the clockmaker — GAVE HIM A "HAND"

52. **Jumbles:** MIRTH FOYER PANTRY COHORT
Answer: His reading of sonnets on the train was known as this — POETRY IN MOTION

53. **Jumbles:** GLEAM TIGER BAKING MARTYR
Answer: How hand-me-down recipes are measured — "GRAM" BY "GRAM"

54. **Jumbles:** EAGLE SUEDE ANYHOW STODGY
Answer: How she pursued her pet's obedience training — DOG-GEDLY

55. **Jumbles:** FUZZY BOWER BUTTON FAÇADE
Answer: What she thought of the airline's price increase — UN-FARE

56. **Jumbles:** POACH EJECT BEHAVE THIRTY
Answer: What they gave her at the hen party — A "HATCH-IT" JOB

57. **Jumbles:** LEECH IMBUE FALTER PURIFY
Answer: Another name for a cattle rustler — A BEEF THIEF

58. **Jumbles:** HOBBY GAUDY FITFUL UNCURL
Answer: How the tiling chore left him — "GROUT-CHY"

59. **Jumbles:** WHEEL DRAFT TRICKY KNOTTY
Answer: What the hamlet called the new arrival — THE TOWN CRIER

60. **Jumbles:** FILMY SOUSE MAGNET BURLAP
Answer: She was unanimously chosen queen because the judges gave her this — ALL AYES

61. **Jumbles:** JULEP CAPON RENDER CHERUB
Answer: What the commuters called the daily traffic jam — CREEP AND BEEP

62. **Jumbles:** SWAMP BULGY REDEEM CAJOLE
Answer: In defeat, a ball game can turn into this — A BAWL GAME

63. **Jumbles:** PLUSH SQUAB MORTAR BLAZER
Answer: What the winning marathon runner lost — HER BREATH

64. **Jumbles:** FRAME FACET DEAFEN FORGOT
Answer: What she called the stockbroker's proposal — A "TENDER" OFFER

65. **Jumbles:** WAGON EXCEL RATIFY CATCHY
Answer: What late snacks give a diet — A FAT CHANCE

66. **Jumbles:** ABASH PRINT POLITE BALLET
Answer: What the miners considered their workplace — THE PITS

67. **Jumbles:** WHISK EMPTY OCCULT DOUBLY
Answer: Why the guitarist never got married — SHE WAS TOO "PICKY"

68. **Jumbles:** VIGIL LISLE LAGOON DAMPEN
Answers: What the spy did to his pursuers — GAVE 'EM THE SLIP

69. **Jumbles:** GAWKY OCCUR CASKET BUBBLE
Answers: What cowboys get for riding broncos — A BUCK OR TWO

70. **Jumbles:** LEGAL DRAWL SHREWD MOROSE
Answers: How the dressmakers described their stern boss — A SEW AND SEW

71. **Jumbles:** CATCH KNIFE PRIMED ENTAIL
Answer: When the chess game ended in a draw they were — FIT TO BE TIED

72. **Jumbles:** PRONE ENJOY ADMIRE EYEFUL
Answer: What the newlyweds called their first trip — A "JOY" RIDE

73. **Jumbles:** TWICE FINIS GYPSUM STUPID
Answer: What the law students studied at the pool — SWIM "SUITS"

74. **Jumbles:** YACHT FUROR KISMET FESTAL
Answer: How the geologist liked his drinks — ON THE ROCKS

75. **Jumbles:** BASIS EXILE FLURRY PAYING
Answer: What autumn leaves might be called — FALL-IAGE

76. **Jumbles:** GIVEN RURAL AVENUE POPLAR
Answer: They trusted the carpenter because he seemed — ON THE "LEVEL"

77. **Jumbles:** MOTIF FEIGN FAULTY SYSTEM
Answer: When he lit up in a No Smoking area he left others — FUMING

78. **Jumbles:** GNOME WEDGE HOTBED MAMMAL
Answer: What the kids did at the park — THEY "GAMBOLED"

79. **Jumbles:** BRIAR CANAL BUOYED PALATE
Answer: How they fed the flames of love — "TINDERLY"

80. **Jumbles:** BIRCH AUGUR BABIED VACUUM
Answer: What they called the baker who sold them stale bread — A BIG CRUMB

81. **Jumbles:** SNOWY LATHE ISLAND ORCHID
Answer: How the silhouette artists described their work — BY A SHOW OF HANDS

82. **Jumbles:** DOWNY BALMY KINDLY BRAZEN
Answer: What they called their daily ocean stroll — THE BORED WALK

83. **Jumbles:** POUCH SURLY JAGGED VISION
Answer: What the orange squeezers exchanged — JUICY GOSSIP

84. **Jumbles:** SAVOR SILKY RANCOR APPEAR
Answer: What the golfers thought their outfits gave them — "SOCKS APPEAL"

85. **Jumbles:** LAPEL PARTY EASILY SEPTIC
Answer: How the roofer trained his apprentice — STEP BY STEP

86. **Jumbles:** AGLOW DOGMA BARREL POLLEN
Answer: What they called the cow in their front yard — A LAWN "MOO-ER"

185

87. **Jumbles:** PANIC TYPED JUNKET THRUSH
Answer: What the struggling violinist did —
KEPT HIS CHIN UP

88. **Jumbles:** BRINY TRAIT TAMPER FERVID
Answer: The miner struck this — PAY DIRT

89. **Jumbles:** JERKY BEFOG AGHAST PREACH
Answer: What she got from the electrician's bill —
AFTER SHOCK

90. **Jumbles:** FROZE BALKY ADDUCE LIQUOR
Answer: Another name for the sleeping bovine —
A BULL "DOZER"

91. **Jumbles:** WELSH CROAK POTTER CANKER
Answer: What a guy who doesn't like having time on his
hands should get — A POCKET WATCH

92. **Jumbles:** JERKY CRESS IMBIBE PURPLE
Answer: What the talkative customer said to the bored
bartender — PLEASE "BEER" WITH ME

93. **Jumbles:** TANGY DOGMA DEBATE BLAZER
Answer: What the doctor charged to fix up the guy who
injured his elbow and knee — AN ARM & A LEG

94. **Jumbles:** NOISE SHEEP DEPUTY NEGATE
Answer: That story about the dog with the wagging tail had
this — A HAPPY ENDING

95. **Jumbles:** COLIC QUOTA OUTLAW FLURRY
Answer: The gondolier may be serenading you, but he's
ready for this — A "ROW"

96. **Jumbles:** AMITY BRASS NEWEST PLOWED
Answer: What a procrastinator has — A WAIT PROBLEM

97. **Jumbles:** EXPEL CABLE FETISH HAZARD
Answer: A "greasy spoon" is a restaurant where you can eat
this — "DIRT CHEAP"

98. **Jumbles:** WHOOP CHIDE COLUMN FIXING
Answer: Language used by those pretentious jet-setters —
HIGH-FLOWN

99. **Jumbles:** MOUND WHINE GARISH FUTURE
Answer: What a shotgun wedding is a case of —
WIFE OR DEATH

100. **Jumbles:** GULLY ELDER DENOTE WOBBLE
Answer: That oil tycoon sure was this! — "WELL"-TO-DO

101. **Jumbles:** GAWKY ELATE CALICO GAMBIT
Answer: What you might find plenty of in a burned-out post
office — BLACK MAIL

102. **Jumbles:** AZURE TAFFY NEEDLE FAMOUS
Answer: What the lazy butcher was — A MEAT LOAFER

103. **Jumbles:** WEIGH BOWER BEHEAD CORRAL
Answer: What one bird said to the other — "WIRE WE HERE?"

104. **Jumbles:** SUEDE JUMPY FATHOM CRAYON
Answer: What the aggressive feline was — A "PUSHY" CAT

105. **Jumbles:** GUEST THICK METRIC ABUSED
Answer: How the eye doctor might make your life —
A "SIGHT" BETTER

106. **Jumbles:** KNOWN DRONE BOTANY PEPSIN
Answer: What skiers get instead of athlete's foot —
SKI "TOW"

107. **Jumbles:** QUILT CRAZY BEAGLE FENNEL
Answer: Coming closer — could it be "in range"? —
"NEARING"

108. **Jumbles:** AGLOW DAISY MEMOIR VANISH
Answer: What you get if you eat too much —
A "HANG OVER"

109. **Jumbles:** CABIN TWEET JUSTLY CROTCH
Answer: What you often have to do to stay within your
budget — WITHOUT

110. **Jumbles:** MOUSY EMERY QUENCH MAMMAL
Answer: What the Pharaoh who ate crackers in bed was —
A CRUMMY MUMMY

111. **Jumbles:** FEWER QUAKE BUNION WHOLLY
Answer: This is terrible — but a letter would make it legal —
AWFUL ("l-awful")

112. **Jumbles:** OWING PRIZE COSTLY MUSEUM
Answer: "What do you serve here?" — "SOUP TO NUTS"

113. **Jumbles:** QUIRE BASSO DECEIT LAWFUL
Answer: "ORATE"

114. **Jumbles:** COVEY GUMBO WALNUT OXYGEN
Answer: "ELBOW" (elbow room)

115. **Jumbles:** PORGY GLUEY INJURE UNFAIR
Answer: Where the short sprinter was unexpectedly
successful—IN THE LONG RUN

116. **Jumbles:** HANDY BRAVE TYPIST PALACE
Answer: There's an extra letter amid "shuffled" papers—
maybe! — PER-H-APS

117. **Jumbles:** SHYLY OCTET PRAYER EITHER
Answer: What usually happens when people marry in haste?
— THEY ELOPE

118. **Jumbles:** BEFOG LIMBO ANYONE LIQUOR
Answer: What the dentist's favorite dish was — "FILLING"

119. **Jumbles:** BERYL SAHIB AUTHOR GENIUS
Answer: The tax people take what they have! — "THE-IRS"

120. **Jumbles:** BULGY TRYST DOUBLE FEMALE
Answer: How to relax completely — "REST-FULLY"

121. **Jumbles:** FORAY VIXEN BISHOP POLISH
Answer: "Yes–it COULD "dispel" pain, sir!" — "ASPIRIN"

122. **Jumbles:** SKULL RABBI ANGINA COMPEL
Answer: A dog that sounds like a boxer — A PUG

123. **Jumbles:** FLORA CROUP TIPTOE CORNER
Answer: What an aggressive businessman stoutly pushed
forward — HIS "CORPORATION"

124. **Jumbles:** MURKY BELIE NOODLE INDOOR
Answer: The egotist's favorite figure — NUMBER ONE

125. **Jumbles:** BEIGE PROVE CALMLY FEMALE
Answer: A dance to wind up with — THE REEL

126. **Jumbles:** WAFER ABATE FAMILY HIDING
Answer: What some investors do when they expect the
market to go down — "BEAR" WITH IT

127. **Jumbles:** OUTDO CLOTH MARAUD GLANCE
Answer: A note of harmony in most households — "DOUGH"

128. **Jumbles:** PECAN MERCY OBTUSE INVOKE
Answer: There is little to see through it — A MICROSCOPE

129. **Jumbles:** TIGER AUDIT REBUKE MOHAIR
Answer: What the medicine man had trouble selling —
A DRUG ON THE MARKET

130. **Jumbles:** BASIN MIRTH FUSION PUDDLE
Answer: Old clothing made from letters — A SUIT OF MAIL

131. **Jumbles:** TRAIT CLOAK ENAMEL GOBLET
Answer: You need a combination of TACT and ART to do this
successfully — ATTRACT

132. **Jumbles:** AWFUL FORTY PROFIT HERMIT
Answer: What cold cash often makes people do —
WARM UP

133. **Jumbles:** ACUTE DAISY PEWTER MUSCLE
Answer: What happened to the baked goods? —
THEY WERE "PIE-RATED"

134. **Jumbles:** WOVEN BASIC DAINTY TEMPER
Answer: What the man who wore two suits to a masquerade
party went as — TWINS

135. **Jumbles:** FUZZY GLOVE BARREN CAMPER
Answer: How to handle a human beast — BE CAGEY

186

136. **Jumbles:** BANJO FEVER LIKELY VANITY
Answer: What the story of the belly dancer was —
A NAVEL NOVEL

137. **Jumbles:** PEACE SAVOR CORPSE MAROON
Answer: This can make a hash of marriage — SCRAPS

138. **Jumbles:** FAITH CHALK RAREFY MODEST
Answer: How the unhappy locksmith sang — OFF-KEY

139. **Jumbles:** AWOKE CURRY TURTLE UNFAIR
Answer: Who the electrician's favorite girlfriend was —
HIS CURRENT ONE

140. **Jumbles:** JEWEL HURRY ORIGIN SYMBOL
Answer: A cover-up in Indiana — "HOOSIERY"

141. **Jumbles:** BOGEY HONEY AROUSE BUTTER
Answer: What they were in the nursery —
HUNGRY AS BARES

142. **Jumbles:** COUGH RUSTY BALLET FUTURE
Answer: What the crazy rower who fell out of his racing boat
was — OUT OF HIS SCULL

143. **Jumbles:** LAPEL BLESS COOPER HAPPEN
Answer: How the banana tycoon lost a lawsuit — ON A PEEL

144. **Jumbles:** BALKY CHAOS ICEBOX LIQUID
Answer: This might be an electric light plant — A BULB

145. **Jumbles:** ADULT INLET WALRUS PLAQUE
Answer: How he produced oil — WELL

146. **Jumbles:** MUSTY ATONE TEAPOT HARDLY
Answer: This might be the latest shoe model — THE LAST

147. **Jumbles:** NOTCH LOUSY NEEDLE MARTYR
Answer: Where you might sit — IN A STAND

148. **Jumbles:** GAVEL BORAX ENZYME LOTION
Answer: The delicatessen man's wife summed up his alibi in
one word — "BALONEY!"

149. **Jumbles:** APART WAKEN CLOUDY BIGAMY
Answer: This kind of strike might cause trouble at the zoo —
WILDCAT

150. **Jumbles:** PANIC GLEAM SURELY UNSEAT
Answer: How the clown in geology class defined "bedrock"
— "MUSIC TO SLEEP BY"

151. **Jumbles:** FAIRY HUMID POTENT TYCOON
Answer: What a guy who got cold feet before the wedding
did — HOTFOOTED IT

152. **Jumbles:** OZONE VITAL IMPEDE POLICY
Answer: A motive for a journey — A LOCO-MOTIVE

153. **Jumbles:** HANDY ACRID CHROME EYEFUL
Answer: Language spoken by the psychiatrist's patient —
"COUCHED"

154. **Jumbles:** JUROR MUSIC DISOWN UTMOST
Answer: Gossip can be a pain when it's this — RUMOR-TISM

155. **Jumbles:** VALUE DOUGH CELERY GUITAR
Answer: What a cravat tycoon might expect plenty of from
the new wide styles — GRAVY

156. **Jumbles:** COLON GRIPE EULOGY LIZARD
Answer: Words that tell you there might be something
unlawful about this sick bird — "ILL EAGLE"

157. **Jumbles:** PANDA KITTY BEYOND GRISLY
Answer: What the pig said as the sun grew hotter —
I'M BAKIN'

158. **Jumbles:** MANLY ENJOY WIDEST SOIREE
Answer: When mother saw the bathroom she said this —
"WATER MESS!"

159. **Jumbles:** HABIT FLOUT BUREAU EMBALM
Answer: This might be THERE in outer space! — ETHER

160. **Jumbles:** PROBE WAGON JAGGED BUNKER
Answer: How you feel after a big weekend — WEAKENED

161. **Jumbles:** FIERCE UNFOLD FALTER SCENIC SIMILE TUXEDO
Answer: When they jogged along the rim of the canyon,
they needed to — EXERCISE CAUTION

162. **Jumbles:** TURNIP SICKEN AFFECT SHRANK GOSSIP HYPHEN
Answer: Everyone loved watching Michael Jordan play at
the — HEIGHT OF HIS CAREER

163. **Jumbles:** GATHER DRIVER ENROLL SHREWD GOALIE CREAMY
Answer: After the kids gave their mom her Mother's Day
presents, she — RAISED CHILDREN

164. **Jumbles:** BITTER URCHIN CHERUB FIASCO EXODUS STIGMA
Answer: Before the cop was done arresting him, the suspect
was ready to — CUT TO THE CHASE

165. **Jumbles:** MEDIUM SHOULD SPIRAL MASCOT NEARLY
BOTANY
Answer: She quit her office job to start her own business
from home, but she — MISSED THE COMPANY

166. **Jumbles:** FIASCO HAIRDO GROWTH TWELVE ASYLUM
MODEST
Answer: He struggled to lose weight because he always had
— "WEIGH" TOO MUCH FOOD

167. **Jumbles:** THORNY DECENT SCENIC DEPICT RITUAL SALMON
Answer: If you could ask Gen. George Armstrong Custer
about his last battle, he'd say he — COULDN'T STAND IT

168. **Jumbles:** HEAVEN GASKET URCHIN ASTRAY SYSTEM INDUCT
Answer: Getting fired for being a rude and obnoxious waiter
— SERVED HIM RIGHT

169. **Jumbles:** DRESSY ICONIC TRUANT FEMALE ORATOR SPIRAL
Answer: What the astronauts wished they had for watching
TV in orbit — SPACE STATIONS

170. **Jumbles:** COLONY COWBOY VOYAGE BUFFET PLIGHT
ROTARY
Answer: What giving birth was for the new mom. —
A LABOR OF LOVE

171. **Jumbles:** ZITHER SEETHE FORKED AUTUMN MAGNUM
ARMORY
Answer: What he got when he paid to enter the marathon.
— A "RUN" FOR HIS MONEY

172. **Jumbles:** ACTUAL VIRTUE INSIST DINGHY WHOLLY HOMING
Answer: Keeping your spending under control often means
this. — GOING WITHOUT

173. **Jumbles:** MISERY SAILOR FORGER HALLOW POETRY INNING
Answer: What the fitness instructor turned into. —
A PERSONAL TRAINER

174. **Jumbles:** SURETY BOUNTY MAINLY EVOLVE BAKERY WALNUT
Answer: The novice bookie suffered tough times because he
didn't — KNOW ANY "BETTOR"

175. **Jumbles:** FIXING MARVEL SCENIC PENMAN CUDDLE FALTER
Answer: Where airline and fighter pilots end up. —
ON DIFFERENT "PLANES"

176. **Jumbles:** MARROW ANGINA VISION INTONE ALBINO EULOGY
Answer: Naturally, a beaver has a — "GNAWING" AMBITION

177. **Jumbles:** EFFORT BOTHER RAVAGE LAWFUL QUARRY
ENCAMP
Answer: The taxi driver said the rainy day was — "FARE"

178. **Jumbles:** INHALE HERESY BUNKER MOTHER MEADOW
BEATEN
Answer: Why the oil baron didn't show his wealth. —
IT WAS BENEATH HIM

179. **Jumbles:** BOUNCE SURTAX DUPLEX MIDDAY MISHAP
ENCORE
Answer: He refused to visit the nudist camp because he was
— CLOTHES MINDED

180. **Jumbles:** CUPFUL NAUSEA METRIC GIMLET QUAINT EMBARK
Answer: When the couple reconciled, they said the marriage
counselor was a — "MAKEUP" ARTIST

Need More Jumbles®?

Order any of these books through your bookseller or call Triumph Books toll-free at 800-888-4741.

Jumble® Books

More than 175 puzzles each!

Cowboy Jumble®
• ISBN: 978-1-62937-355-3

Jammin' Jumble®
• ISBN: 978-1-57243-844-6

Java Jumble®
• ISBN: 978-1-60078-415-6

Jet Set Jumble®
• ISBN: 978-1-60078-353-1

Jolly Jumble®
• ISBN: 978-1-60078-214-5

Jumble® Anniversary
• ISBN: 987-1-62937-734-6

Jumble® Ballet
• ISBN: 978-1-62937-616-5

Jumble® Birthday
• ISBN: 978-1-62937-652-3

Jumble® Celebration
• ISBN: 978-1-60078-134-6

Jumble® Champion
• ISBN: 978-1-62937-870-1

Jumble® Coronation
• ISBN: 978-1-62937-976-0

Jumble® Cuisine
• ISBN: 978-1-62937-735-3

Jumble® Drag Race
• ISBN: 978-1-62937-483-3

Jumble® Ever After
• ISBN: 978-1-62937-785-8

Jumble® Explorer
• ISBN: 978-1-60078-854-3

Jumble® Explosion
• ISBN: 978-1-60078-078-3

Jumble® Fever
• ISBN: 978-1-57243-593-3

Jumble® Galaxy
• ISBN: 978-1-60078-583-2

Jumble® Garden
• ISBN: 978-1-62937-653-0

Jumble® Genius
• ISBN: 978-1-57243-896-5

Jumble® Geography
• ISBN: 978-1-62937-615-8

Jumble® Getaway
• ISBN: 978-1-60078-547-4

Jumble® Gold
• ISBN: 978-1-62937-354-6

Jumble® Health
• ISBN: 978-1-63727-085-1

Jumble® Jackpot
• ISBN: 978-1-57243-897-2

Jumble® Jailbreak
• ISBN: 978-1-62937-002-6

Jumble® Jambalaya
• ISBN: 978-1-60078-294-7

Jumble® Jitterbug
• ISBN: 978-1-60078-584-9

Jumble® Journey
• ISBN: 978-1-62937-549-6

Jumble® Jubilation
• ISBN: 978-1-62937-784-1

Jumble® Jubilee
• ISBN: 978-1-57243-231-4

Jumble® Juggernaut
• ISBN: 978-1-60078-026-4

Jumble® Kingdom
• ISBN: 978-1-62937-079-8

Jumble® Knockout
• ISBN: 978-1-62937-078-1

Jumble® Madness
• ISBN: 978-1-892049-24-7

Jumble® Magic
• ISBN: 978-1-60078-795-9

Jumble® Mania
• ISBN: 978-1-57243-697-8

Jumble® Marathon
• ISBN: 978-1-60078-944-1

Jumble® Masterpiece
• ISBN: 978-1-62937-916-6

Jumble® Neighbor
• ISBN: 978-1-62937-845-9

Jumble® Parachute
• ISBN: 978-1-62937-548-9

Jumble® Party
• ISBN: 978-1-63727-008-0

Jumble® Safari
• ISBN: 978-1-60078-675-4

Jumble® Sensation
• ISBN: 978-1-60078-548-1

Jumble® Skyscraper
• ISBN: 978-1-62937-869-5

Jumble® Symphony
• ISBN: 978-1-62937-131-3

Jumble® Theater
• ISBN: 978-1-62937-484-0

Jumble® Time Machine: 1972
• ISBN: 978-1-63727-082-0

Jumble® Trouble
• ISBN: 978-1-62937-917-3

Jumble® University
• ISBN: 978-1-62937-001-9

Jumble® Unleashed
• ISBN: 978-1-62937-844-2

Jumble® Vacation
• ISBN: 978-1-60078-796-6

Jumble® Wedding
• ISBN: 978-1-62937-307-2

Jumble® Workout
• ISBN: 978-1-60078-943-4

Jump, Jive and Jumble®
• ISBN: 978-1-60078-215-2

Lunar Jumble®
• ISBN: 978-1-60078-853-6

Monster Jumble®
• ISBN: 978-1-62937-213-6

Mystic Jumble®
• ISBN: 978-1-62937-130-6

Rainy Day Jumble®
• ISBN: 978-1-60078-352-4

Royal Jumble®
• ISBN: 978-1-60078-738-6

Sports Jumble®
• ISBN: 978-1-57243-113-3

Summer Fun Jumble®
• ISBN: 978-1-57243-114-0

Touchdown Jumble®
• ISBN: 978-1-62937-212-9

Oversize Jumble® Books

More than 500 puzzles!

Colossal Jumble®
• ISBN: 978-1-57243-490-5

Jumbo Jumble®
• ISBN: 978-1-57243-314-4

Jumble® Crosswords™

More than 175 puzzles!

Jumble® Crosswords™
• ISBN: 978-1-57243-347-2